Darkness
Is My Only
Companion

Darkness Is My Only Companion

A Christian Response to Mental Illness

Kathryn Greene-McCreight

BrazosPress

Grand Rapids, Michigan

© 2006 by Kathryn Greene-McCreight

Published by Brazos Press
a division of Baker Publishing Group
P.O. Box 6287, Grand Rapids, MI 49516-6287
www.brazospress.com

Printed in the United States of America

Library of Congress Cataloging-in-Publication Data
Greene-McCreight, Kathryn, 1961–
    Darkness is my only companion : a Christian response to mental illness / Kathryn Greene-McCreight.
        p.   cm.
    Includes bibliographical references.
    ISBN 1-58743-175-0 (pbk.)
    1. Mental illness—Religious aspects—Christianity. 2. Mentally ill—Religious life. I. Title.
RC455.4.R4G74 2006
362.2—dc22   2005026021

Contents

0991

Preface

This project examines the distress caused and the Christian theological questions raised by a clinical mental illness, namely, mine. This is therefore on the one hand a highly personal book, since it in part tells my own story. Yet it is on the other also theological and pastoral insofar as it deals with questions raised by the Christian theological tradition, such as sin and grace, creation and redemption, God's discipline of the soul, the hiddenness of God, and the dark night of the soul. It also provides practical advice for clergy and friends in dealing with mentally ill folk.

This book has grown for many years. I began writing in the midst of a manic episode in 1998 and returned to composition later, again and again. I have not recounted every episode of every illness, only those episodes that might be helpful to the reader. After all, this book is finally not *about* my own mental illness but my theological reflections on mental illness.

I include throughout the book bits of scripture and quotations from great figures of the Christian tradition to show how the "great cloud of witnesses" (Heb. 12:1) helped, supported, and encouraged me in my illnesses. These are integral to the book, not just frosting. As I state in appendix I, "How I Read Scripture," I drank from scripture throughout my illness in a way that was finally traditional in scope and practice, and healing in promise. The translation of scripture used is the New Revised Standard Version (NRSV), and the translation of the Psalms is from the Book of Common Prayer (1979), except where indicated.

A note on language: I do not, as a policy, adopt "inclusive language" in reference to God. This term disrupts its own definition when we use it for the Godhead. The claim of feminist theologians here is that, as Mary Daly says, "if God is male, then male is God."[1] If Daly's statement is true, then feminists see referring to God in masculine terms as giving patriarchy divine sanction. Therefore, we must not, so the claim goes, use masculine terms or pronouns to refer to God. Many feminists would not use the terms *Father* and *Son*, for example, to speak of the first and second persons of the Trinity.[2] Women, it is said, must be included in the Godhead just as men are.

However, it is not the nature of the Christian God to "include" either males or females within its being in this way. I use inclusive language only for humanity, since there is nothing in the reality of God that allows us, whether male or female, the luxury of being "included" in the first place. Since God is generally referred to in the Bible with the pronoun *he*, this is also the pronoun I generally use to refer to God. I thereby suggest neither that God is male nor that the female is "underrepresented" and the male "overrepresented" in the Godhead.

When you see the word LORD in my text, this points to the Tetragrammaton as in the biblical text, the four-letter unpronounceable name of the God of Exodus 3:14. This will be important in particular in the quotations from the Psalms. Here the name means "He is who He is," or "He will be what He will be," or "He brings into being what He brings into being." It is sometimes transliterated by the word *Yahweh* or *Jehovah* in different translations. *Lord* (capitalized *L* and lowercase *ord*) in the New Testament usually refers to Jesus, along with the pronoun *he*. Clearly Jesus was a man. *Lord* in the Old Testament means something more like "sir" but also can refer to God.

I use the feminine pronoun *she* to refer to the generic patient, the priest, and sometimes the therapist. I use the masculine

1. Mary Daly, *Beyond God the Father: Toward a Philosophy of Women's Liberation* (Boston: Beacon, 1973), 19.

2. Kathryn Greene-McCreight, *Feminist Reconstructions of Christian Doctrine: Narrative Analysis and Appraisal* (New York: Oxford University Press, 2000), chap. 6.

pronoun to refer to the generic doctor, to avoid confusion with the patient. I am not suggesting thereby that women exclusively are mentally ill or that only men are doctors. This is simply a way to use inclusive language in a way that is meaningful for this particular book.

The reader should note that this book is not intended to be a medical manual, taking the place of medical advice. Although it does contain medical information, nothing should take the place of seeing your doctor if you find yourself exhibiting any of the symptoms mentioned. For the full diagnostic criteria of major depression and bipolar disorder, see Kay Redfield Jamison's fine book *Touched with Fire*.[3] See also appendix II below for diagnostic criteria for major depression, bipolar disorder, and schizophrenia.

For those who read drafts of this book and gave me comments, I am grateful: Nancy Brennan, Laird and Sally Edman, Greg Ganssle, Joyce and Robert Greene, Marvin Greene, Steve Horst, Matthew McCreight, Ephraim Radner and Annette Brownlee, Jana and Ron Rittgers, Michael and Carol Tessman. Many thanks to Rodney Clapp for his encouragement, sensitivity, and critical eye. Thanks also to Paul Stuehrenberg from Yale Divinity Library for the Research Affiliates Program, which allowed me the facilities to research this project.

My everlasting gratitude to
Matthew, whose love is beyond measure
Noah and Grace, for their joy
Bob and Joyce, my first theological teachers,
Alex, for her steady friendship
Pam, for her prayers
Barbara, for her strength
For those who were indeed companions in the darkness,
I will always be grateful.

Ad majorem Dei gloriam
et aedificationem ecclesiae.

---

3. Kay Redfield Jamison, *Touched with Fire: Manic-Depressive Illness and the Artistic Temperament* (New York: Free Press, 1993), appendix A, 261–65.

O LORD, my God, my Savior,
  by day and night I cry to you.
Let my prayer enter into your presence;
  Incline your ear to my lamentation.
For I am full of trouble;
  my life is at the brink of the grave.
I am counted among those who go down to the Pit;
  I have become like one who has no strength;
Lost among the dead,
  like the slain who lie in the grave,
Whom you remember no more,
  for they are cut off from your hand.
You have laid me in the depths of the Pit,
  in dark places, and in the abyss.
Your anger weighs upon me heavily,
  and all your great waves overwhelm me.
You have put my friends far from me;
  you have made me to be abhorred by them;
  I am in prison and cannot get free.
My sight has failed me because of trouble;
  LORD, I have called upon you daily;
  I have stretched out my hands to you.
Do you work wonders for the dead?
  will those who have died stand up and give you thanks?
Will your loving-kindness be declared in the grave?
  your faithfulness in the land of destruction?
Will your wonders be known in the dark?
  or your righteousness in the country where all is forgotten?
But as for me, O LORD, I cry to you for help;
  in the morning my prayer comes before you.
LORD, why have you rejected me?
  why have you hidden your face from me?
Ever since my youth, I have been wretched and at the point of
  death;
  I have borne your terrors with a troubled mind.
Your blazing anger has swept over me;
  your terrors have destroyed me;
They surround me all day long like a flood;
  they encompass me on every side.
My friend and my neighbor you have put away from me,
  and darkness is my only companion.

                                                    Psalm 88

Introduction

No testing has overtaken you that is not common to everyone. God is faithful, and he will not let you be tested beyond your strength, but with the testing he will also provide the way out so that you may be able to endure it.

1 Corinthians 10:13

I have struggled with clinical mental illness for the last quarter of my life. In fact, I seem to have had my first depression, then undiagnosed, as a child of twelve years. Minor lows and highs followed throughout my adolescence, but the first major clinical depression was a postpartum episode after my second child was born, thirteen years ago now, when I was in graduate school. That depression lasted a few years, on and off. About five years after that episode, I was diagnosed as manic and therefore bipolar, a disease that bounces between depression and mania. Major depression again followed on the heels of mania, and over the next few years I was hospitalized five times and given two courses of electroconvulsive therapy for major depression. Some five years after I was diagnosed bipolar, my doctor and I finally stumbled upon the right "cocktail" for my brain, and I have steadily improved, avoiding depression and mania since then.

During this time, I have read much of the literature geared to the layperson on mental illness, eagerly searching for a book that would answer, or at least address, my questions: Does God send this suffering? If so, why? And why this particular kind of suffering? Why, if I am a Christian, can I not rejoice? What is happening to my soul?

I found no books among the latest offerings that addressed such questions, and books by Christian authors were often dismissive of the soul's problems in mental illness and of psychotherapy in general. Most of the books answered scientific questions, which were in themselves not uninteresting to me. However, I wanted a book that would ask not purely scientific questions about these illnesses and sets of symptoms but religious questions, and not just any religious questions but a specifically Christian set of questions. What is the problem of suffering and evil viewed from the Christian gospel? How therefore might a Christian respond in the face of mental illness? How is the soul affected by the disease of the mind, indeed of the brain? Does the Christian tradition offer resources for coping with mental illness and for explaining its origin and its healing?

I do not intend to search out and ground philosophical consistency for "solving" the problem of evil; I am no philosopher. I am concerned instead to offer a biblically grounded account, from my own experience, of how the Christian may interpret, accept, and handle suffering, especially that with such a stigma as mental illness. The mentally ill Christian will not be helped much by a philosophical discussion of free will, for example. My concern instead is to offer theological resources for interpreting and surviving mental illness. When I found no book to address my questions, I realized that I myself would have to write it.

This book began, then, as my own agonizing search for the meaning of my mental illness. I hesitated to make this autobiographical; the genre of psychobiography is well represented on the shelves of any bookstore. Instead, I wanted to struggle with the theological meanings, if I could even find any, of mental illness such as my own. How could I, as a faithful Christian, be undergoing such torture of the soul? And how could I say that such torture has nothing to do with God? This is, of course, the assumption within the psychiatric guild in general, where faith in "God" is often viewed at best as a crutch, and at worst as a symptom of disease.[1]

This is only beginning to change, with many studies indicating that religious practice or "spiritual" life can actually help healing of mental illnesses. These studies, however, also indicate that religious people "are less stressed and happier than nonbelievers"[2] and that "religious people are less depressed, less anxious and less suicidal than nonreligious people." This only plays into the caricature of the Christian as perennially cheery. It is a cruel caricature for those Christians who are indeed depressed or otherwise mentally ill. Often they feel guilty on top of being depressed, because they understand their depression, their lack of thankfulness, their desperation, to be a betrayal of God. And yet these studies say nothing of the objectivity of God's involvement in mental illness. How could they, being written by scientists and not theologians? They simply deal with the objectivity of *belief* in God. For many mentally ill Christians, belief in God is no longer objective but becomes subjective, interiorized, and thereby drawn into the circle of doubt. These studies and their apparent outcomes therefore do little toward providing good news to the mentally ill Christian.

How could I, as a Christian, indeed as a theologian of the church, understand anything in my life as though it were separate from God? This is clearly impossible. And yet how could I confess my faith in the God who is "a very present help in trouble" (Psalm 46:1) when I felt entirely abandoned by that God? And if this torture did have something to do with God, was it punishment, wrath, chastisement? Was I, to use a phrase of Jonathan Edwards, simply a "sinner in the hands of an angry God"? What was God doing to me, if it was God's handiwork, and why? Surely the detailed answers to these questions will be as individual for each sufferer of mental illness as is the personal history of each individual and her illness. But these are the questions I wanted to struggle with, partly for my own benefit and partly for the benefit of the body of Christ.

1. See chapter 13 for a fuller explication of the modern mind vis-à-vis ideas of God, in particular for brief theological treatments of the "masters of suspicion," Sigmund Freud, Karl Marx, and Ludwig Feuerbach.

2. Pamela Paul, "The Power to Uplift," *Time*, January 17, 2005, A46.

In an age when we have not only the technology but also the ready habit of attempting to medicate the pains of the mind and soul into remission, these questions have become pressing in a new way. There may be remission, but that is all it is. The shadows and pain of human existence cannot be permanently swept away by medication and therapy; those who have more serious mental diseases such as schizophrenia and bipolar disorder will never be able to come off medications as though finally "cured."

As time went on, however, I realized that could not write such a book as an academic theologian dealing with the problem at an objective distance. This meant, of course, that I had to reveal more of myself than I may have wanted. I decided that I needed to be self-revelatory for the purposes of addressing the questions I list above.

What follows, then, is an attempt to allow the reader enough of a glimpse of my questions as they engage my own experience of the darkness that was often my only perceived companion. The central focus of this book, however, as I hope will be apparent, is not my own experience of the pain but a witness to the working of the triune God in the pain of one mentally ill Christian. Here it will be key to focus on the theocentric rather than the anthropocentric, on the triune God rather than on the self. This may sound backwards. But if I were to focus just on myself, this book would be no different from the many that line the shelves of many bookstores, with their personal narratives of illness and recovery.

For the Christian, the focus of life is not properly the self alone, as an independent agent; rather, the purpose of the Christian life is "to glorify God and enjoy him forever," as the Westminster Shorter Catechism tells us. We are to seek the voice of the Holy One of Israel and heed his call to the body of Christ for obedience and gratitude. How can one then be obedient in the face of a sometimes severe mental disease? How can one praise the God who made the self when that self is in so much pain so as to wish life gone?

I write, then, of my own experience interpreted theologically, with the hope and prayer that this may be of some use to others. It is my way of offering up my own pain to Christ, that it may be redeemed as it touches the lives of others.

Give to us grace, O Father, not to pass by suffering or joy without eyes to see; give us understanding and sympathy; and guard us from selfishness that we may enter into the joys and sufferings of others; use us to gladden and strengthen those who are weak and suffering; that by our lives we may help others who believe and serve you, and project your light which is the light of life.

H. R. L. Sheppard (1880–1937)

This book is laid out in three parts. In the first part, "Facing Mental Illness," I relate my story and attempt to reach out to others struggling with mental illness. In these first six chapters I deal with issues of mental illness in general and my own experience of the highs and lows of bipolar disorder, narrating some of the hardest episodes of my illness and my hospitalizations. This includes my experience of ECT, electroconvulsive therapy.

In the second part, "Faith and Mental Illness," I struggle with specifically theological questions and their bearing on mental illness. In these five chapters, I question the value of the personality and feeling in religious reflection. I also explore the relationship between the brain, mind, and soul, and I discuss the value of prayer for the health of the mentally ill.

In the third and final part, "Living with Mental Illness," I focus on practical issues and advice on how to be a friend to the mentally ill. Since I have used scripture throughout, a summary of why and how I read scripture follows these final chapters. I include an appendix which contains a brief checklist of symptoms for those who are attempting to recognize mental illness. It includes the addresses of some websites that may be useful for the reader.

Part One

Facing Mental Illness

I

Darkness

Affliction is the best book in my library.

Martin Luther (1483–1546)

My thirtieth birthday found me as content as the next person, as happy as I had always been, in fact quite unremarkably normal. I was well adjusted, highly productive, married to the man of my dreams, with an active and healthy toddler, beginning to earn recognition in my chosen field of study. I understood myself to be mentally quite healthy. I had had a stable and happy childhood, blessed with the benefits too often lacking from many other childhoods. The only exception to the streams-of-mercy-never-ceasing was a somewhat unusual series of tragedies that had struck like waves throughout my youth and young adult years. But even these I had weathered well, or so I had always thought.

When I became a mother for the second time, however, the hem of my mental health began to fray. Motherhood by nature challenges the mental, emotional, spiritual, and physical endurance of any woman. It is a highly overromanticized and underestimated pressure cooker, matched in potential not only for the creation of a new family but also for the destruction of both mother and child. Think—with horror—of the Susan Smiths and Amanda Yateses of the world. Smith drowned her two children in a pond by seatbelting them into the car and pushing the car into the water. Yates killed all six of her children, the youngest a newborn, by drowning them in the family bathtub. Of course, not all postpartum sufferers are this detached from reality.

I cannot speak, of course, from experience of the role of the father. I do not mean to discredit his difficulties. I am not aware of the role of the fathers in the Smith and Yates cases. I do know that without the father of my own children, I simply would not have survived thus far. His support and care took the edge off most of my symptoms, especially at this early stage. Without my husband's staunch faithfulness and belief that I would see light beyond this, I simply would not have made it through.

Motherhood, I believe, was only the precipitant for an internal agony that I had been holding back for years. Maybe God had postponed my storm at sea until I could be buoyed by the hope-fulness and joy that I derived from my children and husband. The experience as a whole and the experiences that constituted the eventual illness were at the least bewildering and at most terrifying. The blue sky, which normally fills my heart, stung my soul. Beautiful things like oriental rugs and good food like bean soup absolutely exhausted me. Noise was amplified in my ears, and I fled sound and conversation in search of silence. Small tasks became existential problems: how and why to fold the laundry, empty the dishwasher, do the grocery shopping. My memory failed me. I was unable to read or write (except for sermons, by the Holy Spirit's providence, I believe). And it went downhill from there. A back and forth in and out of darkness lasted for years.

There are many psalms of lament, but Psalm 88 seemed to fit me. It ends in the Book of Common Prayer and in the King James Version with "Darkness is my only companion." Yes, even some of my friends deserted me, except ones who are now the dearest and truest of friends. I was no fun to be with whatsoever, so why not desert me? "What has got her? Why is she in such a bad mood? She can't even remember my name!"

I have a chronic disease, a brain disorder that used to be called manic depression and is now, less offensively, called bipolar disorder. However one tries to soften the blow of the diagnosis, the fact remains that bipolar disorder is a subset of the larger category unhappily called "major mental illness." By the latter part of my thirties, I had sought help from several psychiatrists, social workers, and mental health professionals, one a Christian but mostly non-Christians. I had been in active therapy with a succession of therapists over several years and had been introduced to many psychiatric medications, most of which brought quite unpleasant side effects and only a few of which relieved my symptoms to some degree. Those medications that have in fact been helpful, I must say despite my own disinclination toward drugs, have been a strand in the cord that God has woven for me as the lifeline cast out in my free fall. The medications have helped me to rebuild some of "myself," so that I can continue to be the kind of mother, priest, and writer that I believe God wants me to be. "A threefold cord is not quickly broken" (Ecclesiastes 4:12). The three cords to my rope were the religious (worship and prayer), the psychological (psychotherapy), and the medical (medication, electroconvulsive therapy, and hospitalization).

Yet while therapists and counselors, psychiatrists and medications abound, I found no one to help me make sense of my pain with regard to my life before the triune God. I write this book, then, by way of an offering, as what I wish someone had written to help me make sense of the pain and the apparent incongruity of that agony with the Christian life. Those Christians who have not faced the ravages of mental illness should not be quick with advice to those who do suffer. Platitudes such as "Pray harder," "Let Jesus in," even "Cast your anxiety on him, because he cares for you" (1 Peter 5:7), which of course are all valid pieces of advice in and of themselves, may only make the depressive person hurt more.

This is because depression is not just sadness or sorrow. Depression is not just negative thinking. Depression is not just being "down." It is being cast to the very end of your tether and, quite frankly, being dropped. Likewise, mania is more than speeding mentally, more than euphoria, more than creative genius at work. The sick individual cannot simply shrug it off or pull out of it. While God certainly can pick up the pieces and put them together in a new way, this can happen only if the depressed brain makes it through to see again life among the living. At the time of free fall such a possibility seems absolutely unimaginable. Christians who have not experienced either pole—the high of mania or the low of depression—must try to accept that this is the case, even if they cannot understand it.

> I loathe my life;
>   I will give free utterance to my complaint;
>   I will speak in the bitterness of my soul.
> I will say to God, Do not condemn me;
>   let me know why you contend against me.
> Does it seem good to you to oppress,
>   to despise the work of your hands
>   and favor the schemes of the wicked?
>
> Job 10:1–3

Job is, of course, the quintessential sufferer in the Bible. He suffers immensely and yet always brings his complaint before God. Even when God seems to have abandoned him, Job continues to pray "Do not condemn me . . ." Even though he speaks "in the bitterness" of his soul, he recognizes that he is a soul, and that soul, despite the suffering, is related to God. "Does it seem good to you to oppress, to despise the work of your hands and favor the schemes of the wicked?" Even though God seems to favor the wicked, to whom does Job utter his complaint? God.

> Again I saw that under the sun the race is not to the swift, nor the battle to the strong, nor bread to the wise, nor riches to the intelligent, nor favor to the skillful; but time and chance happen to them all.
>
> Ecclesiastes 9:11

When I asked God why this happened, Ecclesiastes answered: Why not? Time and chance happen to all. Why not this time, this chance, and me?

———

Chopping vegetables for a stir-fry. Baby fussing in the background, three-year old running his toy truck between my feet. Suddenly I see on the cutting board, in place of celery, the severed fingers of my baby daughter. Neat, clean, bloodless. I blink. They are gone now, the celery has returned, the baby is still fussing, her fingers still attached to her hands where they should be, the truck still rumbling along the kitchen floor. I turn back to fixing dinner as though nothing had happened.

An effective coping mechanism: pretending everything is all right, pretending nothing upsetting has happened. It had served me well for some thirty years. Now the storage area in my soul for all the hurts that had been pretended away is overflowing. I need help. Before what I sloughed off was just psychological pain; now my brain is playing tricks on me. Darkness is my closest companion. I need something, but I don't know what. I don't even know how to tell if or when I need help. I don't know what it means to let myself be helped. I never ask for help, even on the odd occasion when I recognize my need for help. That is the definition of me: strong. But now I don't sleep well, can't eat, can't read (a problem for a graduate student), draw no pleasure from the little things anymore.

Physical symptoms bother me. I see my general practitioner: must be a sinus infection or the flu, or . . . he runs test after test and concludes from the exam and blood work that there is nothing physically wrong with me. He suggests that I be seen in Mental Hygiene upstairs. I am appalled at the thought, but he convinces me.

———

"Kathryn, from all of the symptoms you have mentioned and from your answers to my questions, I would say that you are in a major depression and that . . ."

I don't hear the rest. A close friend has just been unsuccessfully treated for depression with electroconvulsive therapy. My father and brother had suffered bouts of depression. But I was the cheery one, the well-adjusted one, the happy face of the family. I try to listen to the doctor above the roaring din of my thoughts scrambling to understand, to piece together the meaning of the incidents I had just recounted to him. How could this be and yet I had not even guessed? What does this mean? My head wails, I cannot hear.

———

Kay Jamison's book *An Unquiet Mind* is the story of her life-long struggle with manic-depressive illness and of her career as a psychiatrist specializing in the treatment of mood disorders. Beyond the narrative framework, though, the book does have a thesis (rather unlike William Styron's *Darkness Visible* or Kathy Crosby's *At the Edge of Darkness*). Her thesis is that love pulls one through the suffering. Sounds sweet, almost trite. The kindnesses of strangers and friends, the acceptance of her disease by those who were able, the love of several men who serially played major roles in her healing: love heals.

Why should this seem trite to me? Shouldn't I see this as an authentic, powerful, and appropriate explanation of what pulls us through? Is it just because I am depressed, or naturally cynical, or a theologian? Maybe all those things. But when one looks at the problem of mental illness from a completely secular perspective, her statement (clearly meant to be hopeful and hope-filling) in fact can fill me with more despair than ever. After all, human love can seem particularly unreliable and fleeting. At times it is unattainable, at others inexpressible, and usually for the depressed, human love is unsensed, and indeed nonsense. Of course, for the depressed individual, divine love can be unsensed and nonsense as well. But at least it never fails! "Love bears all things, believes all things, hopes all things, endures all things" (1 Corinthians 13:7). This is true of divine love, and only thereby derivatively of human loves. So "love pulls you through," when it is not tied to the love of God in Christ but to the random kindnesses of people who happen at the moment to be in a better humor than I, is flat. Yet human loves, such as that of my husband, can certainly be a conduit for divine love, even for those who do not recognize love's true source. If it is the love of God that we see in the face of Christ Jesus that is promised to pull us through, a love that bears out to edge of doom even for the ugly and unlovable such as we, then the statement that love heals depression is in fact the only light that exists in the dark tunnel.

This leads me to wonder how people who are depressed and do not have the conviction of God's unconditional love to hold them steady (even when they cannot feel or sense that conviction) can survive depression. Maybe they do not have such a pessimistic (or what I would prefer to call realistic) understanding of human love. But anyhow, I am a Christian, and how will I survive my depression? God, please enable me to survive. I must allow God to touch me through those people who by God's grace are enabled to love beyond mere human capacity. And maybe it is this sort of love to which Jamison refers after all, although she never says so explicitly. Again, the love of my husband is like this, a grace-filled love. I suppose, though, that we should not fail to recognize God's love extended toward us even in the seemingly trite kindnesses of the otherwise potentially unkind. Even in the listening and patient ear of a psychotherapist, yes, even though I am financing the relationship. I must allow for the possibility for God to work through that relationship. I suppose we have to allow for the possibility for God to be active even among those who are not aware of his presence. It doesn't matter whether they know it or not; God is big enough to handle their potential ignorance.

Help me, O Lord, to make a true use of all disappointments and calamities in this life, in such a way that they may unite my heart more closely with you. Cause them to separate my affections from worldly things and inspire my soul with more vigor in the pursuit of true happiness.

Susanna Wesley (1669–1742)
mother of John and Charles Wesley,
and seventeen other children

Why, with my religious convictions about the love and mercy of God, with my belief in the unconditional and free grace of God poured out in Jesus even in spite of my basest longings and actions, why would I not be filled with joy at every moment, eager to greet the day with the love of the Lord? Especially with a new, perfect baby, a little girl, our Grace, born healthy after some twenty weeks of preterm contractions. I had had, from the outside, a happy and comfortable, indeed privileged, childhood: a two-parent family, a stable home, a good education. I was never neglected by my parents, was always given material blessings that most of the world's children do not have. Amazing that someone even in that cushioned atmosphere should end up in my position, struggling on the edge of sanity sometimes. One of my psychiatrists once suggested that my symptoms as a twelve-year-old sounded like a depression arising from post-traumatic stress syndrome. This syndrome is frequently experienced by soldiers who were traumatized by the atrocities they witnessed and committed in war. How could I have had post-traumatic stress syndrome? As a child and young person I did know many people who committed suicide or died in accidents. The symptoms of post-traumatic stress syndrome can look somewhat like those of depression. But still, I read about the woman who, as a child, was the subject of the famous photo of the naked girl engulfed in napalm flames as she ran through the Vietnamese jungle. Now an adult, disfigured and disabled from the burns, she was able to embrace with her remaining arm the weeping, repentant man who had dropped the bomb that killed her family and maimed her for life. She forgave him. *Forgave him.* She leads a productive life. I lead a productive life too, some of the time, but I never faced the atrocities she did. She does not appear to have post-traumatic stress syndrome. How then could I?

I have been challenged by tragedy, but it was always witnessing the tragedy of others, and even now it is witnessing the tragedy of others that I find absolutely unbearable. It sends me into a complete tailspin. One day recently I saw an old man get hit by an oncoming car as he was walking across the street—the thud of his body against the car, the sight of him dropping to the ground, then trying pitifully to rise. I was the first to reach him, the one to drag him back to his car as he attempted to walk away, the one to take his keys and sit with him until the ambulance came. I was shaky for the next few days. Witnessing the tragedy of others is very difficult for me.

I remember the first time I was confronted with death. Other than hearing of grandparents and uncles dying, the first time I was struck with the reality of my own mortality was the week I turned twelve years old. One of my church choir buddies was killed when a tree fell on her in her backyard. She lingered for about a day, but it was clear that she would not pull out of the coma. I don't remember how I felt, but I do remember adopting the habit of crossing off the days on my bedside calendar with a perfect black *X* after that. I was crossing off the days I had that Cindy would no longer have. A strange undiagnosed illness kept me in bed for about a month sometime after that. I suffered head-splitting pain that made me scream out in the middle of the night. I could not keep food down. I remember being quite content to listen to my purple transistor radio in bed all day. My doctor suggested that may have been my first episode of depression, but at the time no one ever considered that.

Between middle school and college, more tragedies rolled over me. My science lab partner in eighth grade, André, shot himself with his father's hunting rifle one night in a fit of despair. That same year, one of my classmate's older brothers, Tim, killed himself, leaving a note indicating that he had reached his potential in life and had nothing more to "do," as though life were a board game that he had prematurely won. When I was sixteen, my first "real" date, Matthew, was in a motorcycle accident. He lingered for a few days, but his head injuries claimed his life. Then there was Gary, the brother of our church youth group leader, killed in a drunk driving accident; Sandy, my gymnastics teammate, killed herself by diving into an empty pool; Brent, a friend from church youth group, shot himself with his own hunting rifle; Glenn, my co-counselor from church camp, threw himself off a cliff in Hawaii, and Sean, a former student, took an overdose. Later, during my fifth hospitalization in Yale Psychiatric Institute, now Yale New Haven Psychiatric Hospital, another childhood friend hung herself while on suicide watch in another mental hospital in the state. This is not even a complete roster, but by this point I was used to it, if such a thing can be said.

But one thing truly terrified me, and that was witnessing my brother's depression. Of course I knew where it could lead. Once when he and I were both home from college one summer, I begged him never to do that, never to kill himself. He refused to promise. He said he just could not make that promise. That meant that every time he became depressed, would be awake knocking about the house at 3:00 a.m., I would be terrified that he would hurt himself. I found myself wanting to scream out, "Just do it, just get it over with and kill yourself if you are not willing to fight! Don't prolong our agony and yours if that is how this will end anyway!" I felt terrible for having such thoughts and feelings.

Yet I did gain some insight from my brother's and father's depressions. They helped me learn how to protect others from my own depression years later. I would come to refuse the self-pity and blaming of others. I learned to remind myself of my belief that life is a gift. No matter how I felt about my own life,

I refused to give in to suicidal thoughts and acts, even though I often ruminated wildly about them. Still, my compassion for my brother was matched only by this anger toward him. He was clearly suffering, and there was nothing I could do about it. Or at least that is the way I thought about it then.

I think that people who have not dealt with such grief, either first or second hand, simply do not know what happiness is, what joy is, because they do not know what the depths of pain can be. It is like this: you cannot know the import of the cross and resurrection unless you have grasped the weight of sin. All those smiley people out there who are always on an even keel have no idea what joy can be seen from the underside, because they have no idea of the really awful pain life can bring. As Augustine said, the hills drive back the water, but the valleys are filled by it (Sermon 27). In the valleys of depression, one can find a "well-watered garden" if one is so blessed. That is, sometimes depression can be a blessing, because one can learn about God through his hiding. That usually only comes afterward, because during depression, as during the flood, the waters of death cover the face of the earth. As with Noah, it is only afterward that the dove can return with the olive leaf in its beak, a sign of blessing. Only after the storm can God set his bow in the clouds as a sign of the covenant.

> Truly, you are a God who hides himself,
> O God of Israel, the Savior.
>
> Isaiah 45:15

Even here, Isaiah does not say, "Truly he is a God that hides himself." Isaiah addresses God directly, even in God's apparent absence. He acknowledges that this absent God is still his own God and the God of his people. And Isaiah acknowledges that God is Savior, even in hiding. *Truly, you are a God who hides himself, O God of Israel, the Savior.*

During a depression, as during Noah's flood, the good providence of God is hidden from view. All I can see is the storm, all I can smell is the dung of my own ark, and all I can perceive is the very wrath of God. And worse than Noah, I have no companions in my ark, just stinky, contentious inner beasts. Darkness is my only companion.

O blessed Jesus, you know the impurity of our affection, the narrowness of our sympathy, and the coldness of our love; take possession of our souls and fill our minds with the image of yourself; break the stubbornness of our selfish wills and mold us in the likeness of your unchanging love, O you who alone can do this, our Savior, our Lord and our God.

William Temple (1881–1944)

Certainly, mental illness manifests itself differently from person to person. Symptoms can differ. Some can't get out of bed, some sleep too much, some can't sleep, some eat too much, some can't bring themselves to eat. So the diseases are not the symptoms. It is not like cancer, where one can cut out the afflicted sections of the body. The symptoms plague the whole body and mind.

I am not necessarily sad when I am depressed. I am not necessarily "down." Sometimes I just have a gnawing, overwhelming sense of grief, with no identifiable cause. I grieve my loved ones as though they were dead and contemplate what their funerals would be like. I feel completely alone; darkness is my only companion. I feel as if I am walking barefoot on broken glass. When one steps on broken glass, the weight of one's body grinds the glass in further with every movement. The weight of my very existing grinds the shards of grief deeper into my soul. When I am depressed, every thought, every breath, every conscious moment hurts.

So what do I do? I try to distract myself. Enduring episodes of depression requires that I expend huge amounts of energy just to distract myself. My work, when I can by sheer force of will overcome the depression enough to engage in work, is solace. Prayer, when I can climb out of the hole depression throws me into, helps momentarily. Of course, theologically speaking, I know it helps more than just momentarily, but that is not the way it feels. Sleeping, while I am sleeping, if I can sleep, helps as an escape. Tasks, busyness, gardening, tidying up: distractions. Mustn't think, mustn't be conscious, mustn't reflect. This escape from consciousness is at the heart of suicidal energy. It is *not* wanting to hurt the self. It is simply wanting *not to hurt*. When I am depressed, it seems that the only way not to hurt is to cease being a center of consciousness.

Distracting myself, though, is itself depressing, to use the term loosely, because I end up feeling that my every action and thought is a futile flight from pain that will never ease up. Of course, I am not always depressed; in fact usually I am no longer depressed at all. But when I am, there is no "other side," no perspective, no reminding myself that this will pass . . . yes, of course I remind myself of this, but it only enters the top of my brain and then flits right out again. It is never a sure and certain knowledge.

Other than my childhood episode with what now has been suggested to have been depression, my first real head-on toss into the pit as an adult was, as I have said, after my daughter Grace was born in 1992. Postpartum depression is not pretty. It is tragic. Every instinct in the mother pushes toward preserving the life of the child. Most mothers would give their own life to protect their babies. But in a postpartum depression, reality is so bent that that instinct is blocked. Lack of sleep could alone make anyone depressed and hallucinatory, but on top of that the new mother has a rush of hormones playing havoc with body and brain. Perfectly good mothers have their confidence shaken by the thoughts and feelings they endure in postpartum depression.

I realize now that after my son Noah was born in 1989 I also was not well, but at the time I was under so much stress that I just did not attribute my ill health to anything except to having entered a doctoral program with a two-and-a-half-month preemie slung across my front. Two months of bed rest for preterm labor prior to Noah's birth, and hospitalizations afterward because of complications with his health, had left me exhausted and dazed. Looking back further, I can remember times in college that I couldn't get out of bed, was incredibly irritable for weeks at a time, when my friends were strained beyond their capacity to bend with my brain chemistry.

Now, by the grace of God and help from psychotherapy and medicine, I have learned how to protect those around me from my depressive episodes and to prevent the shadows from damaging my relationships with family and friends. Some mentally ill folk use the illness as an excuse to lash out at loved ones. Some disown family and friends, either by running away or by severing relationships. Divorce is a ready exit from either side of the marriage when one partner is mentally ill. Especially in the case of bipolar sufferers, manic episodes with their impetuous affairs and drastic overspending can ruin marriages. Some abuse their family verbally and/or physically, blaming them for the sufferings of the self. Thanks be to God that I never was subject to any of this. When I was manic, my therapist kept a tight rein on me, seeing me every day if needed. The same was true when I was suicidally depressed. She even accepted phone calls in her off hours and figuratively held my hand through many a rough time.

My method of dealing with bipolar energies was to dance with my daughter, who would look at me with unbelieving delight, expecting a depressed mommy. I would garden. I would play the piano and sing at the top of my lungs all the show tunes I knew. This got rather loud and annoyed the children. I would avoid stores and thus the temptation to overspend. But being disciplined with oneself during this stage is very difficult; mania is almost defined by lack of discipline.

My method of dealing with depression was not to lash out but to retreat. When I was depressed I would curl up on our bed and sleep. I could sleep at any time of the day or night, and sleep soundly for hours. I would avoid the family, in part because the noise was so painful to me that I could not stand it and in part because I did not want to make others miserable by my presence. I did not understand at that time that my family and friends truly missed me. I later came to realize this and moved my nest from our bed to the living room as I improved. I was silent and still unable to move, but at least I was there, with the children and my husband.

This leads me to a warning about the children of the mentally ill. Children are often very sensitive and perceptive; they understand much more than we give them credit for. Parents must explain to their children what the nature of the problem is, or the children may create scenarios in their minds that are worse than the realities of the situation. They may even blame themselves. My children pretended they were comfortable with Mommy's spiritual, psychological, and physical absences behind the door of the bedroom, but they became absolutely unhinged when I went into the hospital. Grades slipped, moods dropped. My son became more aggressive, and my daughter withdrew. My husband and I were so embarrassed at the hospitalization that we did not even tell teachers at the children's schools. This was a big mistake that at the time we did not recognize.

We had not prepared the children well enough for my first hospital stay and did not share the details with them. Children need communication at times even as horrible as these, but it must be judicious communication. Do not mention suicidal thoughts or gestures. Just something simple. "Mommy is sick. She is very sad. She needs to go to the hospital. She will get better and be home soon. The doctors will take good care of her." Even telling children that "Mommy has a brain disorder" is better than saying nothing, or than saying that her heart hurts. Children have heard about heart attacks and know how serious they are. Don't bring in half-truths for the sake of protecting the children. Speak matter-of-factly, quietly, calmly. Stress that the hospital is a good place for those who are sick.

When the children did come for a visit to the hospital, they became entirely unglued. They didn't like seeing people catatonic, jumpy, uncontrollable, nor did they like seeing me in such a pale state. My son decided deep in his eight-year-old brain that germs had caused these maladies, and he took to washing his hands obsessively for some time after that. He refused to return to visit me in the hospital. Of course I thoroughly understood. If I had been well, I wouldn't have wanted to be there either. Even though my husband had tried to make the whole situation positive by promising Happy Meals afterward, that first visit was not much of a success. However, the children and I did get to cuddle on the couch, which was very reassuring for all of us. Once again I could be Mommy, even at such a low energy point, and they could be children who weren't expected to suck it up for the sake of the outside world.

So family is very important. The support of a loving spouse is very comforting. My husband was the most loving and most patient partner I could ever imagine. I could never have asked for more. I would question how he was putting up with this blob of a me, or with the zippy version, with no in-betweens. The chores of the household fell on him: laundry, cooking, shopping, child minding. And he still had a full-time job, which he had to cut back. He is a helpmate given by the grace of God. What I would have done without his support and encouragement I shudder to think. Maybe my suicidal urges would have become reality: in many ways I owe my life to him.

My mother came to stay with the children and to help run the household while I was in the hospital. I don't remember how long she was with us, but it was not a short stint. She bore the yeoman's burden while I was in the hospital, cooking and cleaning and taking the children to school. This allowed Matthew to get his own work done and kept the children on a fairly even keel. I don't even remember any more than this, because that time is still fuzzy in my memory and according to my psychiatrist it will always be. Some things I remember quite clearly, and others I cannot recall at all.

Not only family but friendship is so important for the mentally ill. I think I might not have crashed so hard after Grace's birth if a particular close friendship had remained an important support in my life. A host of factors, including my symptoms of depression, which ironically she did not recognize even though her father too has bipolar disorder, tested my friend beyond the point of her ability to love me. Having that support knocked out from under me was a blow that I could not absorb at the time. In depression, it is as though you lack shock absorbers for the potholes, so that these make you bottom out easily. Friendship is very important for those with poor mental health, but it is *very* hard to be a true friend to someone in such a condition. It is just too difficult for some people, for some relationships.

> Even my best friend, whom I trusted,
> who broke bread with me,
> has lifted up her heel and turned against me.
>
> Psalm 41:9

One way to help your friends understand is, as with children, to explain calmly and objectively your diagnosis. I told my friend of my illness only years later. How could she want to be associated with such a groaning blob as I was? If I had told her why I was in such a state, I imagine now that she would not have been so impatient with me, but at the time I felt so alone I could not even reach out. I am not advocating telling everyone you know that you are ill; this is a challenge to handle as you see fit. But those who are closest to you should be warned that your behavior is different from usual and will be for a while, until the medicines get sorted out. They may even be able to help you with feedback. Tell your friends when you are on a new medicine and ask them to let you know how you seem after a few weeks. Do you seem outwardly peppier, with more energy, less grumpy?

Being on the receiving side of friendship is another matter, and sometimes a mentally ill person is capable only of the receiving end. Yet it can for this reason be extremely difficult to be the friend of someone with a mental illness. Often they are not very fun to be with, or they are so much fun that it makes you worry. It is hard to stick with a person who has no conversation to make, no desire to go out with you, eat with you, talk to you.

How can friends of mentally ill patients show their support? Personally, I hated having people ask me how I felt, because I was trying very hard to be OK and didn't want anyone noticing that I was not well. This is, however, not the case for everyone. Reaching out to the mentally ill will at least be appreciated as a token of friendship and concern. One suggestion is simply to ask the patient how you can help. What can you do? The most helpful things for me were the meals, the offers to do a load of laundry or take care of the children for the afternoon. Even though I often did not accept these offers because of a misplaced sense of pride, which depression can foster, knowing that someone cared enough to offer was a source of encouragement.

The friends who were present in their concern but did not demand anything of me were helpful. This meant sometimes not communicating for weeks or months, when I was incapable of conversation. During my hospitalizations, I generally asked friends not to visit. I was too embarrassed. I think I would approach this differently were I to be hospitalized again. It might have lessened the monotony for me and also might have helped my friends not to worry so much.

But frankly, I wondered throughout the time whether I had any friends at all. This was not because of my friends but because of the nature of my illness. While in mania, I felt that everyone loved me and found me scintillating; indeed I found myself scintillating. However, in depression you cannot imagine that anyone would really love you, want to be there for you, find you still worthy of friendship and love. Truly darkness seemed my only companion. Of this I was quite convinced.

One very important way to help your friends who suffer from mental illness is to pray for them. The assurance that people were praying for me, since I had so much trouble praying for myself, was a salve. My true friends during this time were the ones I knew were praying for me. It can be very difficult to pray for someone day in and day out, over and over again, especially when you see little improvement, when you feel like a scratched CD uttering the same phrases over and over, like the woman who pounded and pounded on the door of the judge: "Grant me justice against my opponent" (Luke 18:3). Even so, this was so vital for me. I do not mean to say that the *idea* of people praying for me was a great comfort, although I do suppose this is true to an extent. I mean the *fact* that people were praying for me was key in my dealing with my illness. In other words, it is not just that I was touched that people would think of me. Prayer is more than merely thinking of someone, even though it does involve thought. My point here is that I believe in the efficacy of prayer, in God's pleasure at hearing our desires and needs and providing for that which we seek in prayer. That many people were knocking on God's door for me strengthened me in putting up with the disease and sped the healing, even though the full healing was years in coming. Maybe it would never have come if people had not been praying.

2

Mental Illness

Jesus did not come to remove suffering
or to explain it away.
He came to fill it with His presence.

Paul Claudel (1868–1955)

The mentally ill are one of the groups of handicapped people against whom it still seems to be socially acceptable to hold prejudice. Despite the Jane Pauleys, the Brooke Shieldses, the Kay Redfield Jamisons, and other well-known folks who have experienced some form of mental illness, this seems to be as true in the secular world as it is within Christian communities. Why is this? I would suggest that Christian communities still have a fear of the mentally ill. In part they do not understand mental illness, in part there is a false assumption that the Christian life should always be an easy path, and in part the problem of suffering is hard to grasp. In *The Problem of Pain*, C. S. Lewis suggests that suffering is uniquely difficult for the Christian, the one who believes in a good God. If there were no good God to factor into the equation, suffering would still be painful as an experience but ultimately meaningless because

36

random. For the Christian, who believes in the crucified and risen Messiah, suffering is always meaningful. It is meaningful because of the One in whose suffering we participate, Jesus. This is neither to say, of course, that suffering will be pleasant nor that it is to be sought. Rather, the personal suffering of the Christian finds a correlate in Christ's suffering, which gathers up our tears, calms our sorrows, and points us toward his resurrection.

According to the National Mental Health Advisory Council study of 1993, 2.8 percent of the adult population of the United States at that time, or approximately 5.6 million Americans, suffered from severe and persistent mental illness.[1] A quarter of a million homeless people and 200,000 incarcerated people suffered from mental illness at that time. In addition, the National Mental Health Advisory Council estimated that 7–9 million children were suffering from or were at risk for severe, long-term mental illness. According to a National Institute for Mental Health study, 22.1 percent of all adults in any particular year suffer from a diagnosable psychiatric disorder.

Take the 5.6 million with severe disorders, and multiply this by 2.1 (this is the figure the government uses for the average number of other adults in the average-size family). Add these 11.8 million persons to the 5.6 million, and

we see that at the least nearly 17 million Americans are directly affected, in their nuclear families alone, by persistent and serious forms of mental illness. [In addition,] lifetime prevalence rates of psychiatric disorders' were estimated to be between 28.8 and 38 percent. The numbers only confirm what most of us already know: that individuals with serious mental illness are *everywhere*—among us, with us, all around us—and are a lot closer to home than we usually care to acknowledge.[2]

As of 1999, government estimates of the costs of mental illness were well over $200 billion: loss of productivity, lost earnings caused by premature death, and costs of law enforcement.

The three most significant and serious mental illnesses affecting these mentally ill who are everywhere among us are major

---

1. Jay Neugeboren, *Transforming Madness: New Lives for People Living with Mental Illness* (New York: William Morrow, 1999), 29.
2. Ibid., 30–31.

depression, bipolar disorder, and schizoaffective disorder or schizophrenia. Painting in broad strokes, we can say that all of these are marked by lows or highs of energy and pleasure, sleep disturbance, weight gain or loss. Major depression is often marked by a loss of interest in all aspects of life, especially those that normally would cause pleasure, and a presence of excruciating psychic and even physical pain. Bipolar disorder involves cycling back and forth between painful lows and exhilarating or fearsome highs with a bungeelike bouncing, rather like a tennis ball bouncing from ceiling to floor and back again. Schizoaffective disorder may or may not include these symptoms but will generally involve a divorce from reality, which may include delusions, visions, and auditory experiences. Sometimes all the above symptoms will be present in bipolar disorder.

How then does one become mentally ill, to exhibit these sorts of symptoms? There are many theories, but the reigning ones tend to suggest that it is a combination of nature and nurture, that is, one's brain biology or genetic makeup combined with the stresses and traumas of one's life. This means that strategies for combating mental illness will usually combine both psychotherapeutic and medical approaches.

Just one of the therapies used is interpersonal therapy. This is the usual therapist model, and many types of therapies come under this category. Cognitive behavioral therapy might be considered as optimism at work, linking the mind and the brain to retrain thought processes to more productive, positive ones. Psychoanalysis tends to be used infrequently these days as a treatment especially for schizophrenia, although insights from the theory are still used in the treatment of depression and/or bipolar disorder.[3]

Medical therapies include four general classes of antidepressant medications.[4] The SSRIs, or serotonin selective reuptake inhibitors, such as Prozac, Paxil, Luvox, Zoloft, and Celexa, are the newest and most popular class; they encourage higher brain levels of serotonin. Tricyclics, such as Elavil, Anafranil,

---

3. For more information on therapies, see Stanton L. Jones and Richard E. Butman, *Modern Psychotherapies: A Comprehensive Christian Appraisal* (Downers Grove, IL: InterVarsity Press, 1991).

4. Andrew Solomon, *The Noonday Demon: An Atlas of Depression* (New York: Scribner, 2001), 114.

Norpramin, Tofranil, and Pamelor, affect both serotonin and dopamine in the brain. The MAOIs, or monoamine oxidase inhibitors, inhibit the breakdown of serotonin, dopamine, and norepinephrine. Among these are Nardil and Parnate and they are the most dangerous of the four classes of medications because of their side effects, which can be triggered in conjunction with common foods such as cheese, chocolate, red wine, and soy sauce. Atypical antidepressants, which operate on multiple neurotransmitter symptoms, are Asendin, Wellbutrin, Serzone, and Effexor. In addition, sometimes other medications are used with antidepressants—for example, antianxiety drugs like BuSpar and benzodiazapenes such as Valium, Ativan, Klonapin, and Xanax; antipsychotic drugs such as Haldol, Risperdol, Zyprexa, and Geodon; and mood stabilizers such as Lithium, Tegretol, Lamictal, and Depakote. Another treatment for depression and sometimes for bipolar disorder is known as ECT, electroconvulsive therapy; it will be explained below.

What does mental illness actually look like and feel like? How is depression different from just feeling sad or discouraged or blue? I am not the only one, certainly, to try to describe it. In his award-winning book *Darkness Visible*, William Styron writes:

> The pain is unrelenting, and what makes the condition intolerable is the foreknowledge that no remedy will come—not in a day, an hour, a month, or a minute. If there is mild relief, one knows that it is only temporary; more pain will follow. It is hopelessness even more than pain that crushes the soul. So the decision-making of daily life involves not, as in normal affairs, shifting from one annoying situation to another less annoying—or from discomfort to relative comfort, or from boredom to activity—but moving from pain to pain. One does not abandon, even briefly, one's bed of nails, but is attached to it wherever one goes.[5]

Here is another first-person account by Andrew Solomon, from his renowned book *The Noonday Demon*, which describes

5. William Styron, *Darkness Visible: A Memoir of Madness* (New York: Vintage, 1990), 62.

a depression. Notice the role of sleep here. This is very typical
of the depressive.

> I did not sleep much that night, and I could not get up the fol-
> lowing day. . . . I lay very still and thought about speaking, trying
> to figure out how to do it. I moved my tongue but there were
> no sounds. I had forgotten how to talk. I began to cry, but there
> were no tears, only a heaving incoherence. I was on my back.
> I wanted to turn over, but I couldn't remember how to do that
> either. I tried to think about it, but the task seemed colossal. I
> thought that perhaps I'd had a stroke, and then I cried again
> for a while. At about three o'clock that afternoon, I managed
> to get out of bed and go to the bathroom. I returned to the bed
> shivering.[6]

I remember quite well being unable to get out of bed even to
use the bathroom—being in pain because the need was so great,
but still unable to move. Sometimes I would wait so long that
the need would go away as I became dehydrated throughout the
course of the day.

Leonard Wolff, the husband of noted author Virginia Wolff,
kept a diary in which he tells of her illnesses that plagued her
throughout her life. His account points out especially how depressives can be difficult to care for and how it may take much
patience and energy to keep them physically healthy:

> If left to herself, she would have eaten nothing at all and would
> have gradually starved herself to death. It was extraordinarily dif-
> ficult ever to get her to eat enough to keep her strong and well. . . .
> In the early acute, suicidal stage of the depression, she would sit
> for hours overwhelmed with hopeless melancholia, silent, mak-
> ing no response to anything said to her. When the time came for
> a meal, she would pay no attention whatsoever to the plate of
> food put before her. I could usually induce her to eat a certain
> amount, but it was a terrible process. Every meal took an hour or
> two; I had to sit by her side, put a spoon or fork in her hand, and
> every now and again ask her very quietly to eat and at the same
> time touch her arm or hand. Every five minutes or so she might
> automatically eat a spoonful.[7]

6. Solomon, *Noonday Demon*, 50–51.
7. Ibid., 55.

Once I was out to lunch with a friend who knew I was sick and was making his best efforts to get me to eat my soup. "You're not eating. Does it just not taste good?" "Yes," I responded, "I am eating it." The soup remained in the bowl, and I went home feeling full.

Swiss psychiatrist Eugen Bleuler, who coined the term *schizophrenia*, describes mania in Kay Redfield Jamison's book *Touched With Fire*. He happens to link mania with artistic production, as does Jamison. When one is in a depressed state, creative production is nearly impossible, but in even a relatively mild manic state, if the patient has a talent to work with, prodigious creation can be achieved. Bleuler describes the thinking of the manic patient: "The *thinking* of the manic is flighty. He jumps by-paths from one subject to another, and cannot adhere to anything. With this the ideas run along very easily and involuntarily, even so freely that it may be felt as unpleasant by the patient."[8]

The grandiosity of the manic mind is suggested by Edgar Allan Poe, himself afflicted with bipolar disorder. While the depressed mind is flat, lacking energy, the manic mind images itself as captivating, glorious, resplendent. Poe questions how much this state is actually positively related to his genius and ability to write:

> I am come of a race noted for vigor of fancy and ardor of passion. Men have called me mad; but the question is not yet settled, whether madness is or is not the loftiest intelligence—whether much that is glorious—whether all that is profound—does not spring from disease of thought—from moods of mind exalted at the expense of the general intellect.[9]

Schizophrenic or schizoaffective disorder symptoms are described in the following anecdote from *The Autobiography of a Schizophrenic Girl*. Notice that they include both hallucinations and auditory experiences, and the divorce from reality is apparent. The remarkable thing about this book is that Renée reached a healthy enough state to relate her own schizophrenic

8. Kay Redfield Jamison, *Touched with Fire: Manic-Depressive Illness and the Artistic Temperament* (New York: Free Press, 1993), 107.

9. Ibid., 116; Edgar Allan Poe, "Eleanora," in *The Fall of the House of Usher and Other Writings* (London: Penguin, 1986), 243.

experiences, a rare "cure" for people with such a severe disorder as this.

> One day, while I was in the principal's office, suddenly the room became enormous, illuminated by a dreadful electric light that cast false shadows. Everything was exact, smooth, artificial, extremely tense; the chairs and tables seemed models placed here and there. Pupils and teachers were puppets revolving without cause, without objective. I recognized nothing, nobody. It was as though reality, attenuated, had slipped away from all these things and these people. Profound dread overwhelmed me, and as though lost, I looked around desperately for help. I heard people talking but I did not grasp the meaning of the words. The voices were metallic, without warmth or color.[10]

We might wonder why there is so much mental illness of these more serious types. Certainly, there are many theories—biological, environmental, sociocultural—to explain the genesis of mental illness. But that is just the problem: there are many competing theories. If one tries to draw from all of them some insights into the problem of the mentally ill, one might say that it is a combination of nature and nurture.

Genetics bears a strong influence. Mental illness runs in families. As I have said, my brother and father both suffer from depressions. In addition a first cousin made an attempt on his life. One great-grandfather was an alcoholic, and sometimes alcoholics are mentally ill folk who use alcohol to self-medicate. Our family tree holds stories of other eccentrics as well.

In addition to genetics, it is assumed that stress can make any natural tendencies spill over into illness. This is clearly the case with the stress of postpartum depression. Not every mother responds negatively to the stress of the postpartum period; it is assumed that those who are predisposed to this depression are the ones who end up developing the illness when put under the psychic and physical stress of pregnancy, delivery, and infant care.[11]

10. *The Autobiography of a Schizophrenic Girl: The True Story of "Renée"* (New York: Penguin, 1968), 11.

11. Not every case of postpartum depression is as severe as are some of the examples I mention throughout this book. Mothers who experience postpartum symptoms, however, must get immediate psychiatric care with the first sign of illness. Such care will probably include being put on medicine, which is why

So it is clear that most cases of mental illness are a combination of nature and nurture, of brain chemistry and life stress. This would tend to suggest that we take care of our mental health as we are learning as a society to care for our physical health. That is, if mental illness is not only genetically coded, we would do well to take care with the stressors that we put ourselves under. This could mean, among other things, taking greater vigilance when we are under life stress factors and making more ready use of mental health professionals for therapy and clergy for spiritual counsel.

---

help should be sought at first from a psychiatrist and not a psychologist, social worker, or counselor.

3

Temptation to Suicide

I loathe my life.

Job 10:1

According to Kay Jamison Redfield, suicide is the third leading cause of death for nineteen- to twenty-four-year-olds. Globally, she says, it kills over one million per year. This makes it seem as though it must be an attractive alternative to some. Why should one not commit suicide? The answers apparently are obvious to the sane. Why would I want to do such a thing? The desire for self-protection is built in to the healthy human individual. Suicidal desire is, of course, one of the factors that define the line between illness and health. Self-protection is healthy and "normal," while the urge to end one's life is unhealthy and "abnormal."

> Not only is suicide a sin, it is the sin. It is the ultimate and absolute evil, the refusal to take an interest in existence; the refusal to take the oath of loyalty to life. The man who kills a man, kills a man. The man who kills himself, kills all men; as far as he is concerned he wipes out the whole world.
>
> G. K. Chesterton (1874–1936)

Chesterton's is a typical Christian view of suicide as a grave sin, even the gravest of sins. However, it must be said in addition that suicide can be the ultimate act of the mentally ill, whether depressed, bipolar, or schizophrenic, or those suffering other disorders. I cannot imagine someone killing herself unless she were sick, physically or mentally. It is an act born of desperation and incredible pain.

I used to think that suicide was the most selfish act anyone could perform, since it left those behind in such agony, as Chesterton says. I had much experience with being left behind by suicides. Now I see the matter differently, having been suicidal myself. I now think that suicide is the most pitiful act. I am no longer angry with my friends who took their lives; I feel nothing now for them except compassion, pity, and sorrow. It is an act that of course must be avoided at all costs, but for the person who takes her own life, the pain must be so terrible that now I can understand it instead of being angry at the act.

While I was sick, I experienced much suicidal thinking and wishing. This distressed me in itself, since I as a Christian believe life to be a gift from God to be used to the glory of God. But it was as if a tidal wave had hit me and I could not keep it at bay. Why this? Life is a gift; how could I want to return it, ingrate that I am, to the Giver?

———

Trucks bearing down on me as I look to cross the street are eerily inviting. Especially that huge, square-front, flat-nosed eighteen-wheeler. Such a comforting sight. I imagine myself stepping out in front of it as it barrels down the road. Blessed relief.

———

Counting pills. Do I have enough to settle the matter without landing in the hospital emergency room? I either have to do it not at all or have to do it so well that I don't end up half-alive in the hospital.

A bruised reed He will not break,
    and a dimly burning wick he will not quench.

Isaiah 42:3

I am indeed a bruised reed, a dimly burning wick. How did I get this depressed? Collecting, hoarding, storing away one by precious one the pills that are supposed to help my brain, which will relieve me finally from my misery. Imagining: practicing on my wrists. Razor's edge, cool, clean, and sharp, entering the skin I can no longer feel. Curiosity: blood. At least I would know that I am indeed alive. Wrong and right: desire for death and yet for life. How did I get this depressed, this mad?

> Your hurt is incurable,
>   your wound is grievous.
> There is none to uphold your cause,
>   no medicine for your wound,
>   no healing for you.
>
> Jeremiah 30:12–13

Visit this place, O Lord, and drive far from it all snares of the enemy; Let your holy angels dwell with us to preserve us in peace and let your blessing be upon us always; through Jesus Christ our Lord. Amen.

Book of Common Prayer, 140

How can I even think these thoughts? My children, good God, my children. I cannot do this to them, to my husband, to my family. Dear God, hold me through this. I must not, cannot, will not act on this. But I want it so badly sometimes that I shake, I panic, I pace. I must not must not must not.

—

"Promise me, Kathryn, that you will call me whenever you feel you are in danger. Promise me. You may not leave my office until you promise me." My therapist was faithful beyond measure.

—

I heard on National Public Radio the other day that a man in France withdrew his life savings from the bank, the equivalent of twenty-six thousand dollars, and set it on fire in his bathtub. Then he took a bottle of sleeping pills. He was rescued and put into a mental hospital. He now wonders why he did it. I have never been that destructive, thank God. But seeing and hearing things that weren't there made me feel truly crazy. For some reason the garbled, mixed voices, as if at a fuzzy cocktail party, came to me while I was in the kitchen, and rarely elsewhere. I was so depressed that my mind was bent and broken.

What does suicide mean for the Christian? We all remember the days when the Roman Church would not bury a suicide in its holy ground. This is because while suicide is not one of the seven deadly sins (except as it is considered murder), it is considered to be unforgivable by God, so great is the offense. The Christian understands the body to be the temple of the Holy Spirit. "Do you not know . . . that you are not your own? For you were bought with a price; therefore glorify God in your body" (1 Corinthians 6:19–20). Glorify God in your physical body; glorify God in the body of Christ, the community of the faithful. Life is something for which the Christian, both as individual and as community, is bound to give thanks.

Certainly I do not want to be heard as recommending taking one's life in any situation, even in cases that are terminal. For all my suicidal thinking, I *knew* what I believed in the deepest pit; even though I could not feel it, I knew that suicide is wrong. In any case, how do we respond pastorally to the case of the suicide? Can we say that God forgives even here? Do we shun the funeral service of the suicide?

Suicide usually leaves in its wake a family and friends who in the midst of the horrendous pain grope for meaning, for understanding, and they present a case for delicate and loving pastoral care. I would suggest that no death of a loved one is as painful as a suicide. Not only is there the despair of the loved one who committed suicide, but there is also the despair of those who are left with the legacy of their loved one's final act. Sometimes the will is not sufficient to the task of changing despair to joy, even for the Christian.

We must not act on our despair. How so for someone who is suicidal? Borrow from the faith of your brothers and sisters in Christ. Worship regularly, daily if possible, not only in the privacy of personal prayers and devotions: even there, maybe especially there, the devil will be waiting for you, subtly turning you back in on yourself and away from God. Worship in communion with other brothers and sisters in Christ. If praying and praising are impossible for you now, which they may well be, borrow from the prayer and praise of those around you. Clothe yourself in the faith of the saints. Do not be ashamed or afraid to rest on their devotion if you can muster none of your own. "You are not your own, you are the Lord's, you were bought with a price; glorify God in your body" (1 Corinthians 6:20). Lean on the body of Christ. You are not your own; you are not *on* your own. If you cannot praise now, do not let that worry you. There is enough causing you pain without something more agonizing you. What you need to do now is hold on to your hope, even if you cannot access it or find relief in it. Do not act on your despair.

In Nick Wolterstorff's *Lament for a Son*, a moving book by a kind fellow about the tragic death of his own son, there is a passage that has haunted my soul, that I cannot push away, that scars the otherwise thoughtful, indeed beautiful, book irreparably for me:

> The son of a friend—same age as Eric—died a few weeks before Eric. The friend's son committed suicide. The pain of his life was so intense that he took the life that gave the pain. I thought for a time that such a death must be easier to bear than the death of one with zest for life. He wanted to die. When I talked to the father, I saw that I was wrong.[1]

How could anyone even think such a thought? How could someone even dare to whisper such a thought? Even for the purpose of saying that the thought was mistaken: how could such a thing even be said, be written, make it past an editor, and be published? The world understands so little what it means to lose someone to suicide, to handle the loss, to bear the legacy of a suicide attempt, to struggle with the tempting yet false peace of suicide. How little a person must previously have had to struggle with the pain of suicide to think such a thought. And yet this author is a very thoughtful, deeply spiritual man.

I do think a Christian's suicide, especially that of a Christian teacher or pastor, is the final act of disobedience, of betrayal of the Creator. Of course, I know this is often not consciously chosen, or when it is conscious, it is a choice born of tremendously unbearable pain. A friend's pastor suffocated himself in a plastic

---

1. Nicholas Wolterstorff, *Lament for a Son* (Grand Rapids: Eerdmans, 1987), 25.

garbage bag, leaving a whole congregation asking questions such as "What could we have done?" If they had noticed the symptoms, maybe they could have confronted him and begged that he get help, reassuring him that they were all with him. The fact is, there may be nothing they could have done. His death shook them so, more than if he had been simply their boss or business partner. This was the man who had offered the gospel, who had preached words of hope. Yet he committed the ultimate act of hopelessness.

It does seem that the stakes are high: the Christian's suicide in effect contradicts every good word about God one could ever have preached, undoes every good work dedicated to God and neighbor that one could ever have accomplished. I cannot allow myself so to undermine my very life's work. I pray to God for strength to hold on.

4

Mania

Mania is sickness for one's friends, depression for one's self.

Robert Lowell (1917–1977)[1]

D ear God what is happening to me I can't even speak. My mind races races zooms phrases run together ideas bleed what is happening calm down just calm down you are exaggerating. I believe, Lord; help my unbelief. Nothing is wrong. Nothing is wrong. Nothing nothing is wrong. Why is the doorbell ringing ringing who is here dear God who is coming for me who is going to think I am crazy even though I am fine just fine if only my mind would stop racing I am *not* going to any hospital why would Matthew have called them and not told me? You are paranoid. Stop it. Stop it. Stop. No one wants to take you to the hospital. Just Matthew's friend coming over. Paranoia is nothing more than excessive narcissism. Unattractive, unchristian. Why are my teeth chattering why am I hyperventilating I am not cold. Dance. Go dance.

1. Kay Redfield Jamison, *Touched with Fire: Manic-Depressive Illness and the Artistic Temperament* (New York: Free Press, 1993), 249.

Snowstorm. Gorgeous exotic turbulent swirls of snow. Magic. The world tingles. My brain sparkles, all things connect. Panic. Am breathing too fast, am going to choke, am going to lose my vision. I feel drunk but have had no drink. I watch myself move, listen to myself speak as though to another. What will she say? How does her mouth move? What will she do? Panic help someone help me.

Have never found the condiments aisle so fascinating. Never even really thought about condiments: pickles, relishes, sauces. Who would want a vinegared vegetable, after all, when one could have it fresh? But look at all these pickles. Sweet sour dill kosher (how kosher are they really?) peppers onions cauliflowers even eggs baby gherkins slices chunks relishes spreads green red white orange brown all because long ago before refrigeration our papas and mamas had to find a way to preserve the crop for the lean winter months. Of course that is how cheese came to be too, because when you have too much milk but no fridge you get a stinky mess unless you make cheese which itself is a stinky mess but more edible than soured milk, according to most cheese eaters that is. Jars jars jars of pickles.

What was that? Calling my name? Are they coming for me? Am taking too long in the pickle aisle . . . talking to the jars? . . . everybody must be watching . . . someone must have called the manager . . . Oh good they are calling someone else's name . . . but what if that is a tactic to calm me down so then they can pounce on me before I try to run away . . . clever, clever . . . don't be paranoid, the height of narcissism . . . but what if I am right?

Delicious, exhilarating, a rush. I walk six inches off the ground. If I just go a bit faster and jump I will fly.

Mania can be fun at first, but if one goes too high or too fast, the fun ends and the nightmare begins.

What am I doing here in the car? How did I get here? I don't remember driving here. Tears. Breathing too fast again. Should call for help. Calm down. Why do I keep telling myself to calm down? Jesus, where are you? Help me. Holy God, where are you? A very present help in trouble, my foot. Where are you? Have you dropped me again? But I am not depressed, at least that. What is wrong with me?

"Kathryn, can you hear me? Do you hear what I am saying? I think you need to see a doctor. Did you call Dr. K like I suggested? He's really a very nice guy, a very human doctor, the best psychiatrist in New Haven. Nobody doesn't like Dr. K. Kathryn, do you know why this is happening? Look, you need to be seen today. I am calling Dr. K right now."

"You are having a manic episode. I have some medicine that will help. If you start the medicine now, you can prevent the cycle from swinging out of control. I would suggest that we try you on Depakote, which has been used for years to treat epilepsy, and more recently to treat manic depression . . ."

Manic depression? Is that what you are saying I have? This is ridiculous. Look, this is just a silly mistake. B. just overreacted. She's very sweet but a bit overly protective . . . What if I am just exaggerating, making this all up, and you are ready to treat me like I am some epileptic convulsing on the floor . . . I thank you very much for your concern. But I really don't want to take any medicine. . . . For how long? Two days? Five days? . . . *Six months?* Maybe my *whole life?* Who is the crazy one here? . . . This is absurd. You don't even know me. I have always been a little nutty. That is normal for me. . . . So, let me get this straight, you want me to continue the Zoloft to keep me from getting depressed, and take the Depakote to keep me from getting too happy, and take the Ativan to keep me from getting too panicky? You really have a pill for every occasion, don't you? . . . Can I go now? No, I know this is not a prison, but I didn't want to be rude. Yes, I know we aren't really finished, but how are we supposed to reach closure on this one? You want me to take drugs and I don't want to . . . OK look, I really think you are blowing things out of proportion, but go ahead and give me the prescription . . . no, don't call it in, just give me the slip . . . I will talk to my husband about it. He's the one who has to put up with me; he should have some say in all of this.

Almighty God, have mercy upon us, who, when troubled with the things that are past, lose faith, and life, and courage, and hope. So have mercy upon us, and uphold us, that we, being sustained by a true faith that Thou art merciful and forgiving, may go on in the life of the future to keep Thy commandments, to rejoice in Thy bounty, to trust in Thy mercy, and to hope in the eternal life. Grant unto all of us, whatsoever may betide us, to remember ever that it is all of Thy guidance, under Thy care, by Thy will; that so, in darkest days, beholding Thee we may have courage to go on, faith to endure, patience to bear, and hopefulness to hold out, even unto the end—Amen.

George Dawson (1821–1876)

I am damaged. Manic depressive. No one understands this, no one will understand this. Last night someone made a crack at karate class that the brown belts doing their pinyans looked like medication time at the state hospital. They were making a joke at the expense of people not unlike me. There but for the grace of God go I. No, even despite the grace of God go I. And, of course, all of us, but those blokes with their sanity somewhat intact can pretend that it has nothing to do with the grace of God, that fundamentally they are better than the sedated stooges at the state hospital. Dear God, I thought you had humiliated me, chastened me, taught me enough about my frailty and complete reliance upon your sustaining grace. Have I not learned my lessons well enough, that you must teach me yet again? Depression was bad enough, but this is horrifying. To know that without these little pills I might do something mortifying, embarrassing, dangerous. I might think I could fly. Maybe start directing traffic. People simply cannot accept mania. Depressives are nonthreatening, but people are afraid of maniacs.

———

"Mania is often followed by depression. A manic episode often will trigger a depressive episode. We have medicine to help."

———

Medicine. None of this is medicine. Medicine makes one better, cures a disease. These drugs only mask symptoms, and if the drug is removed, the symptom may still be there, or may not, and may return at some future unforeseen point. This is not medicine. These are just pills. Humiliating reminders that my brain has short-circuited.

I desperately do not want to take my medication. Depression is worse than awful, but hypomania, just under the edge of mania, is fun. Before it overflows into full-blown mania, it is remarkable. I am light, quick, brilliant, fascinating even to myself. I watch myself as though I were an actress on the stage. But being medicated for mania is painful, at first, because I don't know the highs and have no excuse for the lows, and I feel dull and dead inside. The medication for mania takes away all the liveliness that I knew in mania. It makes my mouth dry, my bowels stop, my stomach ache. It puts on weight, which was a good thing at first, but later combined with an antidepressant it causes excessive weight gain. This can't be good for my health.

This is the point at which many people throw out the medication, or stop taking it and save it surreptitiously for the suicidal stages. I admit that throughout my depressions over the years that followed, I would garner stockpiles of ammunition like this against myself just in case I could not take the lows. There would follow conversations with therapists and psychiatrists to convince me to dump the arsenal down the toilet. Stockpiling medication is probably one of the most dangerous habits a mentally ill person can fall into. Certainly I could have taken an overdose of ibuprofen for lack of anything else, but that would not have been as dangerous as an overdose of antidepressants or antimania medication. If you know of anyone who is depressed or manic, make sure as possible that they are not stockpiling medication for future reference. All medicine that is not being used at present should be thrown out. Convince them to give it to you, and flush it down the toilet. Don't put it in the garbage where they can retrieve it.

In the end, there were two factors that kept me from taking those arsenals, even though I desperately did want to at certain points. I knew what it is to survive a suicide, and I knew that my children would simply never recover and that my husband would be devastated. I could not do that to them. As close as I may have come, I could not do that to them. I never wanted to hurt myself or anyone else, I just desperately wanted to end my suffering. Still, I never let my children's welfare out of my sight.

Other than my family, who I might say were a passive influence on me, since they were not aware at the time how much danger I was in, the active influence on me was my therapist. A petite woman, she has the emotional strength of a Sisyphus and used it to wrestle me out of the most dangerous times and to push me, ever up and inching down the hill again, finally back up to health. While I know that she would say it was my work, not hers, this is the way I see it.

So, during mania, I felt completely different from the way I did at the depressive pole. Mania doesn't hurt the way depression does. Depression meant that every breath, every thought, every moment of consciousness hurt. Every particle of my consciousness ached, throbbed, stung. Mania was the opposite: every breath, every movement, every image before my eyes, every thought sparkled, glittered magically, filled me with ecstasy. Centrifugal motion, bliss.

At this point, thanks to the medicine, I am not filled with ecstasy. Neither am I in agony. I just want to end my existence. I am tired—not physically, no, because the medicine is working. Heaven forbid I should be physically tired. Leave it to American medicine to make a drug that provides productivity even during depressive episodes. But I am tired of existing inside of myself, I don't want to be inside my own skin, am tired of feeling and talking and figuring out why I feel this way and that way, tired of putting off the inevitable, that I should return to the earth from which the muddy Adam was shaped.

5

Darkness, Again

O Lord, help us not despise what we do not understand.

William Penn (1644–1718)

After mania comes the darkness, again. The doctor's medicine has managed to build a ceiling for the mania, to keep me from traveling too high. But there is as yet no floor for the depression. I am in the subbasement, bungeed from high to low. With the darkness, I experience visions and voices. This is true of mental patients from time to time. But the stigma of mental illness, including the jokes made by the healthy about the ill, is worse than the visions and voices. At least the visions and voices teach me something about myself and about God. But the stigma teaches me nothing except about the proclivity of humanity to harm humanity. Working despite the realities of this stigma, there are many who have suffered mental illness and yet were and are prodigious in their fields. This gives me hope: I want to be one of these prodigious ones as well, despite the stigma of mental illness.

Darkness, again. It comes and goes over the next several years. After five weeks on the Depakote, after I have swung from mania to depression again, the doctor wants me to try Lithium. Apparently that works well with one of the antidepressants I have not yet tried, Wellbutrin. But first I have to get on the Lithium, then get on the Wellbutrin, then come off the Zoloft that I have been on for four years. This whole process will take about a month. Sometime in that series of events I will come off the Depakote. Good. I can't stand it. Every time I forget to take the Depakote I start feeling normal again. Why am I taking this stuff? I do hate these drugs, yet I have to give them a try. For the sake of my family I must try to put up with this. Just try my best to stay out of the hospital. Do whatever I can to try to get better so as not to be hospitalized. I have a theory about these drugs: the doctors give you this medication that makes you quite sick, and the result is that you resolve never again to complain about any of the symptoms! Hey doc, good to see you, I am feeling just fine. See you next week . . . I sometimes have very little faith in their "medicines."

Darkness, again. This titrating of medicines will last for years, on and off, as my depressions flow from low to lower and low again. The trial of each medicine will take at least several weeks before we know whether or not it will work. One will last for a few months, leaving me only mildly depressed at best, and then it will "wear out." Then we will try another, and the side effects will be impossible to endure. Then we will try another, and the side effects will be impossible, but it is the only medication to make me significantly better. We layer medications throughout, trying to find the perfect cocktail for my brain. Through all this time, the mania is under control and the depression is the plague.

> Discipline yourselves, keep alert. Like a roaring lion your adversary the devil prowls around, looking for someone to devour. Resist him, steadfast in your faith . . .
>
> 1 Peter 5:8–9a

Tell me about it. But if I were to say this to any of my doctors, I imagine they would think this was paranoia, a symptom of my disease. Is it? I don't think so. Sometimes I do think the roaring lion is a symptom of my disease, or maybe that my disease is wrought by the devil. My doctors would regard this as magical thinking—another symptom of disease. There are some things I simply cannot discuss with them. Religious experience is not something many of them are at all willing to take into account.

> There is therefore now no condemnation for those who are in Christ Jesus. For the law of the Spirit of life in Christ Jesus has set you free from the law of sin and of death.

Romans 8:1–2

Help me, Lord, to remember this, to chew this cud, to digest it, to take it into my very heart, to carve it on the very stone of my heart. Christ Jesus has set me free from the power of even these illnesses.

You really can't make jokes in a mental hospital. You have to be careful about what you say, because the doctors may take you seriously and think you are sicker than you really are. And you can't even mention that you have to be careful, or they will think you are paranoid. A sign of mental illness. Or am I just being paranoid?

> Abide with me; fast falls the eventide;
> The darkness deepens, Lord, with me abide;
> When other helpers fail, and comforts flee,
> Help of the helpless, Lord, abide with me. . . .
>
> I fear no foe, with thee at hand to bless;
> Ills have no weight, and tears no bitterness.
> Where is death's sting? Where grave, thy victory?
> I triumph still if thou abide with me.

Henry F. Lyte (1793–1847)

Darkness, again. Today as I was driving home from my teaching job at a small New England college, the road started going up in smoke before my eyes. Curling up like a burning page. *Abide with me.* The doctor says that during profound or prolonged depressions, this sort of thing can happen: I see things that aren't really there, I hear things that others don't hear. At seventy miles an hour, watching the road roll up like a scroll before one is, to say the least, startling. But the vision expressed the way I feel: the way ahead of me is disappearing but I am hurtling nevertheless into the void. Of course I should not have been driving in this state. But even the mentally ill need to go where they need to go, just like the rest of the world.

> Peace I leave with you; my peace I give to you. I do not give to you as the world gives. Do not let your hearts be troubled, and do not let them be afraid.
>
> John 14:27

As I was planting some seeds, carefully poking them down into the soil and covering them lightly, I heard the verse "For you have died, and your life is hidden with Christ in God" (Colossians 3:3). Like the seeds hidden snug under the soil, waiting for the powers of nature to change them into sprouts, my life is hidden with Christ in the life of the triune God. I am not yet what I will become—thank God this is not "as good as it gets"! I am protected through the merciful layer of God's shielding of my life from all that would destroy it. And there is so much that seeks to tear my life away from God these days. There is the depression, the mania, the efforts to overcome the depression, and the desire to allow the mania's tornado winds in my mind and my soul. But despite all that I desire and all that I do not desire, both poles of the spectrum which would exclude the Holy One, my life is hidden, protected, nurtured in God, in spite of myself. Such words of comfort. And to think I am taking medication to keep such voices at bay. God can work even despite the medication.

Suffering is not eliminated by the resurrection but transformed by it. "I consider that the sufferings of this present time are not worth comparing with the glory about to be revealed to us. For the creation awaits with eager longing for the revealing of the children of God" (Romans 8:18–21). The resurrection gives us hope for the future. "The creation itself will be set free from its bondage to decay. . . . For in hope we were saved. Now hope that is seen is not hope. For who hopes for what is seen? But if we hope for what we do not see, we wait for it with patience" (Romans 8:21, 24–25). In the resurrection of Jesus, death will be no more. The resurrection will kill even the power of death and promises that God will wipe away every tear on that final day. We still have tears in the present. We still die. In God's future, however, "death, thou shalt die" (John Donne, 1572–1632). The tree of life in that ancient Garden becomes the cross that gives us life. This is the notion of Christian hope: the resurrection of Jesus is the first fruits of the promise of the general resurrection, when we will be raised to joyous life with God.

The hope of the resurrection is not just optimism, and it leans the Christian life ever facing toward the future, not merely dwelling in the present. The Christian hope is not only for the individual Christian, nor only for the church itself, but for all of creation, which was bound in decay by that first sin: "Cursed is the ground because of you . . . thorns and thistles it shall bring forth for you" (Genesis 3:17–18). This curse of even the land and its increase will be turned around at the resurrection. All creation will be redeemed from pain and woe. Of course, for the mentally ill, this understanding of Christian hope gives comfort and encouragement. Sorrowing and sighing will be no more. Tears will be wiped away. Even fractious brains will be restored.

> Save me, O God,
> for the waters have come up to my neck.
> I sink in deep mire,
> where there is no foothold;
> I have come into deep waters,
> and the flood sweeps over me.
> I am weary with my crying;
> my throat is parched.
> My eyes grow dim
> with waiting for my God.
>
> Psalm 9:1–3

Darkness, again. Prayer now is screaming, writhing, panting, hissing curses through clenched teeth. Who is this God who curses me first, and in return, sends a cycle of curses?

> Be angry but do not sin; do not let the sun go down on your anger . . .
>
> Ephesians 4:26

Angry, yes, that is my life's song these days. To know that scripture recognizes that we get angry, and allows the expression of anger, is a great comfort. And how psychologically healing that it would say to express anger but not to let it spend the night with us.

> Where can I go from your spirit?
> Or where can I flee from your presence?
> If I ascend to heaven, you are there;
> if I make my bed in Sheol, you are there.
> If I take the wings of the morning
> and settle at the farthest limits of the sea,
> even there your hand shall lead me,
> and your right hand shall hold me fast.
> If I say, "Surely the darkness will cover me,
> and the light around me become night,"
> even the darkness is not dark to you;
> the night is as bright as the day,
> for darkness is as light to you.
>
> Psalm 139:6–11

Even if I don't see you, don't want to see you, feel you have abandoned me, want to abandon you, even there you are with me. This I can feel only after coming out of Sheol. But I look back and know you were there. Darkness is not dark to you. Even though I may feel that darkness is my only companion, to know that the darkness and the light are alike to you is great comfort.

Spring should come soon.

While the mentally ill cannot make jokes around their doctors, people make jokes of those who are mentally ill. The reality may be funny to others, but to those who are mentally ill, not much of this is very funny. An advertisement I saw on a billboard in a train station showed a rock climber dangling from a rope, with the text "What's this maniac doing? He forgot his sunscreen." This was by the American Association of Dermatologists. Valentine's Day of 2005 brought the "Crazy for U" teddy bear wearing a straitjacket. The National Association of the Mentally Ill registered a public complaint. The 1927 silent film *Jeanne d'Arc* has a scene in which it is said that this movie was "discovered" in the closet of a mental institution. While watching this, a whole crowd laughed, except for me, of course. I reckon that people think mental patients are off their rockers, completely detached, unbalanced. While that may be so for some at times, it is not necessarily so. Mental patients are suffering; they are not funnier than anyone else. I think people laugh and think ill of them because people are nervous and uncomfortable with the very notion, for after all, sanity is a thin veneer on many folk. The difference between many "normal" and "ill" is that the ill folk have to admit their illness. Jokes only promote the stigma.

The worst thing about mental illness, besides the pain, is this very stigma. The taking pleasure from others' pain. The jokes. Stigma creates a fear on the part of the mentally ill and cycles the fear of those who are healthy against those who are ill. I was so ill that at times I couldn't move and yet didn't want to tell my boss why I couldn't come in to work. I had supervisors and colleagues, then, whom I never told. I realize now that I should have done so, but at the time I didn't trust them with the news that I had a mental illness—one that would plague me for life. How could I go back to work after revealing that news?

Indeed writing this book is risky business. Stigma against the mentally ill can be so strong. How will people trust my intellectual and spiritual capacities if I once had difficulties with my memory, personality, and even speech and muscle control? If I actually thought the unthinkable, to take my own life? I am a priest, a public speaker, a writer and theologian. How could I ever go back to my work? How would I be trusted by my senior rector, by my parish, by my bishop, by my colleagues in the academy? One friend, a professor of theology, actually said about another friend who had been through electro-convulsive therapy (ECT), "His career is finished." Obviously I never told her about my own problems. And so although I was hospitalized five times, most of my employers did not know. My bishop knew that I was ill, and was very understanding. Most just thought I was oddly unreliable, or unreliably odd.

One thing to recognize about mental illness is that it does not necessarily mean the sufferer has a characterological fault or personality disorder. It may mean this, but never meant this in my case. The sufferer of mental illness may be the kind of person you might still want for a friend, not an insidious, manipulative, lying cheat, for example. Part of the tragedy of stigma is that people do not understand that the mentally ill can be quite normal in many ways.

Many prominent people throughout history actually were mentally ill but during their stable times conquered the stigma and produced prolifically. I think of William Cowper (pronounced Cooper, 1731–1800), the poet and hymnwriter who wrote "O for a Closer Walk with Thee," "Jesus, Where'er Thy People Meet," "God Moves in a Mysterious Way," and many others. At more than one point he attempted unsuccessfully to take his own life, and he was committed to a psychiatric hospital for a time. It is said that John Newton, his friend, pastor, and collaborator on some of the hymns, the author of the famous "Amazing Grace," saved Cowper from suicide more than once. Cowper and Newton together wrote many hymns familiar to us today. Because of Cowper's mental illness he was not able to hold down a job, yet he produced a profound hymnody and poetry. Even those who scorned evangelicals as "Methodists" would read Cowper's poems and sing his hymns. He addressed many social problems, such as the African slavery of his day, as did Newton.

> God moves in a mysterious way,
> His wonders to perform;
> He plants his footsteps in the sea
> And rides upon the storm.
>
> Ye fearful saints, fresh courage take;
> The clouds ye so much dread
> Are big with mercy, and shall break
> In blessings on your head.
>
> Judge not the Lord by feeble sense,
> But trust him for his grace;
> Behind a frowning providence
> He hides a smiling face.
>
> Blind unbelief is sure to err
> And scan his work in vain;
> God is his own interpreter,
> And he will make it plain.

The sense that God's storm clouds are great even with mercy, that his frowning providence hides a smiling face, that God is the interpreter of his own work are themes that give comfort to the depressed soul. Mercy is hidden in the storm; God's smiling face hides behind the frown of providence. So even the hiddenness of God can be a comfort.

Christina Rossetti (1830–1894), also a hymnwriter and poet, suffered too from mental and physical illness, yet this did not slow her down during her more healthy times, and even while she was sick she was actively writing. She authored, among many other works, the carol "In the Bleak Midwinter."

> In the bleak midwinter, frosty wind made moan,
> Earth stood hard as iron, water like a stone;
> Snow had fallen, snow on snow, snow on snow,
> In the bleak midwinter long ago.
>
> Our God, heaven cannot hold him, nor earth sustain;
> Heaven and earth shall flee away, when he comes to reign;
> In the bleak midwinter, a stable place sufficed
> The Lord God almighty, Jesus Christ.
>
> Angels and archangels may have gathered there,
> Cherubim and seraphim throngéd the air;
> But his mother only, in her maiden bliss,
> Worshiped the beloved with a kiss.
>
> What can I give him, poor as I am?
> If I were a shepherd, I would bring a lamb;
> If I were a wise man, I would do my part;
> Yet what I can I give him?—Give him my heart.

Again comes through the notion of the hiddenness of God as paradox even in the incarnation, the high point of the revelation of God: neither heaven nor earth can hold God, and yet a stable will suffice to enclose the Babe.

Rossetti, writing under the nom de plume Ellen Alleyn, was hailed by the public as a literary success. Her first public poems appeared in the *Athenaeum* when she was only eighteen. Her writings reflect her deep religious devotion: she was a high church Anglican and a follower of Tractarianism (the Oxford Movement, a conservative catholic position). As a girl, Rossetti had been passionate, vivacious, and quick-tempered even to the point of self-harm: she once cut herself with scissors after being punished for a minor offense. As an adolescent, she contracted an unexplained illness with physical and mental symptoms. Her religiosity was called into question as cause or symptom of her illness. After she returned to health, Rossetti became even more intensely devoted to her religious observance. The questions I have are these: Why was her religiosity impugned as being inappropriately severe? How does one determine such a thing, and who is to determine it: psychiatrists or priests? Are psychiatrists qualified to make such a judgment?

> The strong are not always vigorous, the wise not always ready, the brave not always courageous, and the joyous not always happy.

These are the words of Charles Haddon Spurgeon (1834–1892), the great nineteenth-century preacher in London, who fought depression and severe anxiety throughout his lifetime. Yet he kept on preaching throughout his illnesses, both physical and mental. His output of sermons was prodigious over the course of his fifty-seven years, totaling some 3,500. He also authored 135 books, and this was all from a man who hated writing.

"Depression comes over me whenever the Lord is preparing a larger blessing for my ministry. It has now become to me a prophet in rough clothing. A John the Baptist, heralding the nearer coming of my Lord's richer benison." Clearly Spurgeon felt about his depression much as I do about mine. Out of it comes a blessing, even though while in it not much but agony can be perceived. In this sense, God sends suffering in order to teach. "If the Christian did not sometimes suffer heaviness he would begin to grow too proud, and think too much of himself." This comment is open to criticism from secular therapists, who generally understand depressives to have a poor self-image. "But you must think more of yourself and leave your depression behind, Spurgeon," they might say. That is clearly not the way he saw the situation.

Word has it that the Niebuhr brothers, Reinhold (1892–1971) and H. Richard (1894–1962), also suffered from depression. They were both considered among the finest American theologians and ethicists of their day, Reinhold teaching at Union Seminary in New York and H. Richard teaching at Yale Divinity School in Connecticut. Among some of H. Richard's famous books are

Christ and Culture, Meaning of Revelation, and *The Kingdom of God in America*. H. Richard spent time in the same hospital where I did. His younger brother, Reinhold, wrote among other works *The Children of Light and the Children of Darkness*, *The Interpretation of Christian Ethics*, and *The Nature and Destiny of Man*, and is the usually uncredited author of the famous Serenity Prayer now used by Alcoholics Anonymous the world over. He is also the author of this famous triad:

Nothing that is worth doing can be achieved in a lifetime; therefore we must be saved by hope.

Nothing we do, however virtuous, can be accomplished alone; therefore we are saved by love.

Nothing which is true or beautiful or good makes complete sense in any immediate context of history; therefore we must be saved by faith.

In fact, a long train of famous and creative artists have struggled against mental illness and succeeded in overcoming the stigma. According to Kay Redfield Jamison in her book *Touched with Fire*: *Manic-Depressive Illness and the Artistic Temperament*, a whole crew of prolific artists shared more than simply talent. They also suffered from mental illness: Charles Baudelaire (1821–1867), Samuel Taylor Coleridge (1772–1834), Hartley Coleridge, his son (1796–1849), Emily Dickinson (1830–1886), Gerard Manley Hopkins (1844–1889), Victor Hugo (1802–1885), John Bunyan (1628–1688), Charles Dickens (1812–1870), Ralph Waldo Emerson (1803–1882), Graham Greene (1904–1991), Mary Shelley (1797–1851), Georg Friedrich Händel (1685–1759), and many other brilliant artists suffered from either depression or bipolar disorder. Many of these cases were complicated by self-medication with the likes of alcohol or opium. Of course for most of them psychiatric medications were not yet available. Just some contemporary examples of prolifically talented mentally ill are Art Buchwald, Rosemary Clooney, Dick Cavett, Jane Pauley, Kay Redfield Jamison, and Mike Wallace.

Many other famous highly creative people could not bear their mental illness and took their own life: Sylvia Plath (1932–1963), Anne Sexton (1928–1974), Ernest Hemmingway (1899–1961),

Virginia Wolff (1882–1941), and Vincent Van Gogh (1853–1890), just to name a few. Each of these individuals contributed to our culture and society despite their illnesses. I wonder how many of them, had they lived, would have produced more beautiful poetry, prose, music, and art. And I wonder in how many cases today society is being robbed of great productivity and creativity because of mental illness. Mental illness is not a death sentence on one's work, especially in these days of improved medications, if it is treated promptly and effectively. And the fact that these others have overcome the stigma of mental illness gives me hope for myself and my own work.

Christian hope means that time is important. The Christian life is not just a circular spinning into nothingness but drives toward the goal at the end of time, the divine healing of all creation. Time bears its purpose out in bringing us ever closer to the will of God in the redemption of creation. But in my darkness, yet again, I have learned something about time and mental illness. This is still hell, just unrelenting hell. That is because time stands still. The essence of being depressed is the stillness, the molasses-in-January thickness of time. It is like the inverse of the saying "Time flies when you're having fun." Time does fly during manic streaks, but my depressive black holes are just the darkness and void of nothingness, not even the movement of time. If time moved, maybe I could get somewhere, get out even if only inch by agonizing inch, out of this muck. In the midst of this sluggish hanging of time, all I can do is hold on and ask God to abide with me in the void. If only time would even crawl rather than slither, I would be in less agony. *Abide with me.*

I try to remember that it is the creeping slowness of time that allows the crocus to push its way through the frozen earth. If the crocus moved any faster, it would destroy itself in its struggle against the ice. And the slow but sure movement of the crocus is a sign of the end of the winter. Maybe the slowness of time then is God's mercy. I just have to remember that.

> The peace of God, it is no peace,
> But strife closed in the sod.
> Yet, Christians, pray for but one thing:
> That marv'lous peace of God.
>
> William Alexander Percy (1885–1942)

God's strange gift of time. Depression can be seen as a form of intensely painful boredom. There is no future to look forward to, only to dread, and the past terrifies, haunts. When time rolls by, it doesn't even touch you. There is no melancholy for the passing of time, just furtive wishing it away, to be rid of it, to be drowned in its billows instead of carried aloft, eagerly expecting the next wave of goodness. Time for the mentally ill is stuck. It is not a gift but a curse. Yet at the very beginning of time, even before God creates the sun and stars to mark time, God creates "evening and morning, the first day." Time is a gift of God to create the space for our living of our days before the Creator. Depression subverts this knowledge.

Time even enfolds itself, plays back on itself, drops off the cliff of present experience. Sometimes one can in a flash go into a deep depression, as though the lights in the room were suddenly turned off. Some eight years after my postpartum depression began, we were traveling in Guadeloupe. We left our darkened, cool room, and the second I stepped outside I was stricken with a profound depression. The exotic birds, the gorgeous flowers and plantings, the blue sky, the sandy beach, the very fact that we were on vacation suddenly made me sick to my soul. The birds were miserable, the flowers stank with rottenness, the blue sky washed gray, the white sands dimmed green, and the idea of the relaxation of vacation distressed me unbearably. Everything struck me as pain. Unfortunately this did not turn off as quickly as it turned on, and I was left in yet another depression for many long months following. Even after the ECT, after rounds and rounds of medication and hundreds of hours of "talk" therapy, I kept falling into the darkness, again.

Come, Lord Jesus, you for whom darkness is as light, remove this veil from my face and enable me to see you.

> Come my Way, my Truth, my Life,
> Such a Way as gives us breath,
> Such a Truth as ends all strife,
> Such a Life as killeth death.
>
> George Herbert (1593–1633)

6

Hospital

Lord Jesus Christ, you are for me medicine when I am sick;
you are my strength when I need help;
you are life itself when I fear death;
you are the way when I long for heaven;
you are light when all is dark;
you are my food when I need nourishment.

Ambrose of Milan (340–397)

I had been taking many different medications in a series,
trying to find the ones that would "work." This was five
years after my postpartum depression, which never really
went away permanently. Only many years after that, with the
combination of the last four medications, have I felt truly better. I have tried the following in differing constellations and
combinations: Prozac, Paxil, Atavan, Luvox, Zoloft, Celexa,
Wellbutrin, Serzone, Effexor, Buspar, Depakote, Topamax,
Zyprexa, Geodon, Parnate, Ambien, Lamictal, Abilify, and
Nardil, with Lithium almost throughout. At times the medicine felt less like weapons against depression and mania and
more like Saul's heavy armor on the young David. They made

69

me shake, quiver, sleep, then lose sleep, confused, disoriented, amnesiac, unable to pronounce even my own name. I would fall asleep anywhere, including at the wheel when driving or when standing at prayer. The confusion has been one of the worst problems for me. I once had such a level head. It felt as though I could have fought better at times without the side effects, and as David chose to take off his armor, so I once or twice chose to come off my medication. I got immediately worse. The armor went back on.

Some of these medications can be dangerous, in particular Nardil and Parnate. They require a strict diet, devoid of cheese, chocolate, red wine, caffeine, smoked meats, and soy sauce, to mention just some of the offensive items. I have on more than one occasion ended up in the hospital emergency room with blood pressure alarmingly high from a reaction to a dangerous food. There was risk of both stroke and heart attack. Thank God I was preserved from these. While I have found the MAOIs to be critically useful, they are risky to take.

The other day I read a text from the Babylonian Talmud (completed sixth century A.D.) that said that the cure for depression is to eat red meat broiled over coals and to drink diluted wine. This sounds no more absurd than taking antidepressants, the specific function of which the medical world really does not know.

During my depression after Guadeloupe, I became increasingly sick while trying drug after drug that had no effect. I was in so much psychic pain that I could not bear it. My therapist suggested the hospital; I immediately rejected the idea. A mental hospital? Maybe for other people, for the weak, but not for me. I was embarrassed and ashamed just at the mention of the idea. My first therapist had brought it up as a possibility that might be helpful when I had postpartum depression after Grace was born. This was some five years later, but I was still adamant about not going to the hospital. However, over months of agony, my defenses against the hospital broke down, and I finally agreed to enter what was then called Yale Psychiatric Institute for an as-yet-undetermined amount of time. The stay ended up being short, just about a week.

> Out of the depths I cry unto thee, O Lord!
> Lord, hear my voice!
> Let thy ears be attentive to the voice of my supplications!

If thou, O LORD, shouldst mark iniquities,
Lord, who could stand?

But there is forgiveness with thee,
that thou mayest be feared.

I wait for the LORD, my soul waits,
and in his word I hope;
my soul waits for the LORD
more than watchmen for the morning,
more than watchmen for the morning.

O Israel, hope in the LORD!
For with the LORD there is steadfast love,

And with him is plenteous redemption.
And he will redeem Israel from all his iniquities.

Psalm 130 RSV

Waiting on the LORD when one is mentally ill takes extreme effort. Yet the soul does wait for the LORD more than watchmen for the morning, with that dead-tired heavy expectation of the sun's inevitable rise. Yes, even though I was not sure that the sun would really rise, that the LORD would really come. It was only through reading the Bible and the prayers of others, in particular the Psalms, that I came to be able to wait, to hope in God's plenteous redemption. Or at least to acknowledge that some had that hope and that I wanted to be in the community that had that hope, even if I could not feel it.

O LORD, my heart is not lifted up,
my eyes are not raised too high;
I do not occupy myself with things too great and too
marvelous for me.
But I have calmed and quieted my soul,
like a child quieted at its mother's breast;
like a child that is quieted is my soul.
O Israel, hope in the LORD
from this time forth and for evermore.

Psalm 131 RSV

Like a child quieted at its mother's breast. I love that image. I remember when my son, my first child, was an infant, he would get so hungry and grumpy, but within seconds of his latching on to the breast, the grimace would leave his face and a flood of delight would spread over him. A child quieted at its mother's breast. Dear God, give me your milk and quiet my soul; give me the peace of feeding on you.

Teaching. At college, in the classroom. What in God's name am I doing here, up in front of all these people? What if I melt down here in front of them? I am supposed to be going to the hospital today, and here I am leading a discussion in front of some ninety college students.

My therapist, B., called to say that I had two options: either the geriatric ward at Yale–New Haven or the adolescent ward at Yale Psychiatric Institute. I said that we should just forget the hospitalization thing. Just forget it. She didn't agree to that plan. During the day, a spot opened for me on the adult unit at YPI.

Again, my mother was visiting to help out at the time. Told her that B. wanted me in the hospital. As calmly as if I were saying that I was going to the store for milk. Inside I was a mess. Mom had no idea this was a real possibility, because I had successfully been convincing her I was well. Mom gave a pained yelp, asking if it had really gotten that bad. Yes, I replied, turning and quickly walking away. Can't stand the pain I cause others; the pain I cause myself is too much in and of itself. Packed my suitcase. Had set out most of what I would need the previous night, so this was quick. Asked Mom to drive me. Didn't want her with me when I checked in. Couldn't bear to see her face, hear the worry in her voice.

The thing about the hospital: you can block out the world. You don't have to respond to people if you can't, and they won't take offense. If you can't handle your family's worry, you can just cut it off, just like all the external stresses: lift the needle off the record. That is what the hospital was for me.

> I loathe my life;
>> I will give free utterance to my complaint;
>> I will speak in the bitterness of my soul.
>
> Job 10:1

Yes, Job, I understand how you could loathe life. Certainly I understand. But how can I loathe the life given me by a good

Creator? This has got to have an element of evil. Clearly of sickness, of illogic, of twisted thinking. Yet I do not actively participate in this. I try to participate actively in prayer, in the exercise of faith, hope, and love. I pray daily, and this helps immensely. But it is all removed from me, as though through a sound-proof, bulletproof glass. I am alone. Darkness is my closest companion.

Bring us, O Lord God, at our last awakening into the house and gate of heaven, to enter into that gate and dwell in that house, where there shall be no darkness nor dazzling, but one equal light; no noise nor silence, but one equal music; no fears nor hopes, but one equal possession; no ends nor beginnings, but one equal eternity; in the habitations of your glory and dominion, world without end.

John Donne (1572–1631)

There is light. Would that I could go there now. But it is more worthy to stay here for your benefit: my husband, my children. How could I do this to you—rush God's grace, usurp it, and reach into the heavenly places, only to choose in reality the darkness? How could I do that to them? Simply, they would never recover. I must not, I must not, I cannot, but I want desperately to be removed from this pain. I don't want to kill myself, just to be relieved of this darkness, emptiness, lack of care. Sleep. Sleep is one way out. Sleep just for a while, to face it all over again upon waking.

My husband, Matthew, just wants to help. He keeps asking me what he can do. He says that he feels so helpless. He is helpless, and so am I. There is nothing he can do. Yet maybe there is. I tell him not to treat me like an invalid. When I can't get up, when I can't crack a smile through my plaster mask of a face, when I can't do anything but weep, just hold my hand. *But please don't be in pain for me.* Because then I can see that on your face, and it makes my pain worse. Just treat me in a matter-of-fact way: Kathryn is depressed again. Or when I am manic, don't get scared of me. Don't get mad at me just because I talk too much, have too much energy, burst at the seams with ideas for the garden, the house, vacations, books. It is not my fault that I swing from one extreme to the other. I know loving me right now is a big challenge. But that's how I can be helped.

How firm a foundation, ye saints of the Lord,
is laid for your faith in God's excellent Word!
What more can he say than to you he has said,
to you that for refuge to Jesus have fled?

"Fear not, I am with thee; O be not dismayed!
For I am thy God and will still give thee aid;
I'll strengthen thee, help thee and cause thee to stand,
Upheld by my righteous, omnipotent hand.

"When through the deep waters I call thee to go,
the rivers of woe shall not thee overflow;
for I will be with thee, thy troubles to bless,
And sanctify to thee thy deepest distress.

"When through fiery trials thy pathway shall lie,
My grace, all sufficient, shall be thy supply;
the flame shall not hurt thee; I only design
thy dross to consume, and thy gold to refine.

"The soul that to Jesus hath fled for repose,
I will not, I will not desert to its foes;
that soul, though all hell should endeavor to shake,
I'll never, no never, no never forsake.

John Rippon (1751–1836)

This hymn would always make me cry when I was depressed.
I always wondered, what did my parish think as I wept during
many of the hymns? But no one ever confronted me. Maybe
they never noticed? Or maybe they were too embarrassed for
my sake to ask, too polite. "That soul, though all hell should
endeavor to shake, I'll never, no never, no never forsake." I felt
entirely forsaken, but God's promise in Christ to me was over-
whelmingly comforting.

———

Walked into YPI on my own, suitcase in hand. Apparently they
are not used to seeing this. The security guards at the entrance
thought I must be lost. "This is a hospital," they said, as though
I didn't look like a potential patient. Emergency room shuntees,
or those forcibly admitted by family or friends, but someone

alone? A fairly attractive, sane-looking woman (for all intents and purposes of their evidently dulled imagination) couldn't belong here. They were amused. I was not.

———

After this Job opened his mouth and cursed the day of his birth. Job said:

> Let the day perish in which I was born,
>   and the night that said,
>   "A man-child is conceived."
> Let that day be darkness!
>   May God above not seek it,
>   or light shine on it.
> Let gloom and deep darkness claim it.
>   Let clouds settle upon it;
>   let the blackness of the day terrify it.
> That night—let thick darkness seize it!
>   let it not rejoice among the days of the year;
>   let it not come into the number of the months.
> Yes, let that night be barren;
>   let no joyful cry be heard in it. . . .
> For my sighing comes like my bread,
>   and my groanings are poured out like water.
> Truly the thing that I fear comes upon me,
>   and what I dread befalls me.
> I am not at ease, nor am I quiet;
>   I have no rest; but trouble comes.

Job 3:3–7, 24–26

Bags checked before I could enter the locked ward—somewhat like at the airport, but even more stringently than after 9-11. Searched for any item with which I might harm myself. They removed from my belongings my mirrored compacts and my pencil sharpener. Implication: I might use these to harm myself. Why then didn't they confiscate my belt, my shoelaces? They frisked me, made me disrobe just to make sure I was not concealing something. What? A razor blade? A hedge trimmer? Lawn mower, maybe, tucked neatly into my bra? For sure. They didn't make me remove my brain. That's the only thing that could harm me now.

Interviews with nurses, doctors. Some of the patients do make this place look like a nuthouse, to use an unfortunate term. I am among the most "normal" looking of them, whatever "normal" means here. Funny that I should look normal. But I suppose I do. I am still thin, soon however to gain weight in the pattern of most patients who are on heavy psychiatric medication. I dress in jeans that fit, without the derriere hanging out or the stomach peeking through. I put my hair up in a clip because it is dirty: depression makes taking a shower feel like climbing Mount Everest. Many patients stay in their pajamas all day. I will come to that, too, after a few days. My face and arms are clear of the cigarette burns and other self-inflicted wounds of many of the other patients. I speak my educated talk, while most of the patients are less schooled than I. Why? I wonder. My religious life also separates me from the others, who for most part think my concern with prayer must be a psychological glitch. Yet I appear "normal," like one of the staff. But just look inside my mind, and that would disabuse you of the idea that I am normal. My favorite line: "Do you work here? You don't look like a patient."

Ate dinner on the ward. Tuna sandwich. Not yet allowed off the floor. On fifteen-minute checks. Every dashed fifteen minutes they wake me through the night to make sure I am still alive and not trying to harm myself. This is so terribly humiliating, but I know I have to go through with it. For the sake of my family. For me? Can't get there right now. Another favorite line of the day: "Why are *you* on fifteen-minute watch?" Again, I am a good actress. The first time I got checked at night, I started and sat straight up in bed. "Oh nothing, just checks," said the nurse. I learned to sleep through them as time went by, and eventually they took me "off" them.

In the Yale Psychiatric Institute, they do not generally manacle people except in the most severe cases of agitation. It is not like the movies. That is because most people there are not in the condition that would call for it. This sort of treatment happens more in the emergency room, if for instance one is in a manic state or tripping out or otherwise uncontrollable. I have never had to endure this. But I imagine that it would be completely embarrassing and angering.

YPI is somewhat like a hotel, in a way, just a hotel that you can't leave anytime you want. Someone once likened the hospital to a place where you have security but no privacy. The wards are locked. At mealtimes they take us downstairs, one worker ahead of the fifteen or so patients, and one behind. They count the group at the top of the stairs and count again at the bottom. The cafeteria is unlocked for our entry, and locked again behind us. The food is not bad; I was expecting poor institutional fare.

The floor I was on had some eight or ten bedrooms, mostly doubles, with two quads. There was a room with a piano and large table where activities took place. A pay telephone was our only link to the outside world. Cell phones were not allowed. There were three bathrooms on the floor for the patients, and laundry machines. There was a small eat-in kitchen that opened on to the large gathering space. Weighing in was the first routine of the day for those of us who were underweight. There was a living room at the end where we shared goals. This was one of the groups, indeed sometimes the only group among those that I was well enough to attend, that bordered on therapy. At the beginning of the day and then again at the end, goals were set, and then in the evening the day was evaluated as to how we reached them or not.

My goal was always to say the Daily Office, something that took only twenty-five minutes twice a day in the "real world" but in the hospital and in my ill brain took most of the day. This lent new meaning to the phrase *"Daily* Office." Reading the psalms, collects, scripture, and prayers was nearly impossible. Concentration was no longer a possibility, and each word seemed to swim in front of my eyes. But I was determined that this should be part of my therapy, even if my doctors seemed a little concerned about my "religiosity." Overly religious speech and ideas can be a sign of "ill health."

Sometimes, very occasionally, there was art therapy. I remember making a clay vase and being so calmed by the silky texture of the clay, and almost tickled that I had actually made something that pleased me. There were staff-led games to keep the better-off among us from sheer boredom. There were sometimes other therapy groups, and an exercise class.

The chaplain came around two days a week or so. She was an extremely warm and compassionate woman whom I had known previously from our church affiliations. Upon seeing me, she exclaimed, "And what are you doing here?" Not the best way to greet someone who already feels ashamed about being in the hospital. It seemed that her job consisted of leading the Spirituality Group, which I attended only once. It was only generically religious. Her other task was to fill out information forms on each patient. Home address? What religion? What church/synagogue? Name of religious leader? When she asked if there was anything she could do for me, I asked her to pray with me. She did, quite willingly, but then never offered again.

Laughing Christina. She hears voices almost constantly and laughs, even at the most inappropriate times. Might be nice to hear such amusements. Better than hearing voices that make you weep or scream. Laughing Christina. Then there is Sophie, the old woman in the wheelchair who is convinced that the staff is getting ready to kill her, and pleads quietly with me to tell her what they are planning. Douglas, who at group meetings spells his name when called on, D-O-U-G-L-A-S, and lets out a belly laugh, gleeful. He does not say much else. Steven, who is so depressed that his vocal cords do not function. Daniel, whose wife left him because she just could not bear his depression. The others fade into forgetfulness.

They let us out of the building after meals into the courtyard, the unbreachable fortress walls surrounding us and keeping us "safe." Fresh Air Run, they call it. Instead of running, the patients would stand around and smoke. Stale Air Slouch.

At one point when I was hospitalized, maybe the first or second time, there was actually a gym with exercise bikes that they took us to on occasion. I always went when the opportunity arose. The bikes were old and useless, but even the short walk to the gym was a relief of sorts.

Almighty God, whose most dear Son went not up to joy but first he suffered pain, and entered not into glory before he was cruci- fied: mercifully grant that we, walking in the way of the cross, may find it none other than the way of life and peace; through Jesus Christ our Lord.

Collect for Friday, BCP, 99

Today is Friday March 13. My childhood friend Cindy was killed by the falling tree on a Thursday-the-twelfth. Ever since then, I am not afraid of any Friday-the-thirteenth. Superstition is, of course, completely antithetical to biblical faith. But I don't even need to get that far. Tragedy strikes even on the days when you don't expect it. Why scout it out by setting apart certain days to be afraid?

> Be my strong rock, a castle to keep me safe.
> you are my crag and my stronghold.
>
> Psalm 71:3

This hospital is God's castle to keep me safe. A place where I cannot hurt myself, where I am protected from my own brain, where God has tucked me away from the stresses of my life. I can sleep. I can zone. I can completely avoid talking to anyone, except of course the doctors and social workers. I don't have to pretend here. Christ is my castle to keep me safe. He has entered the hell of this place for me, gone before me, and stays with me.

———

An alternative therapy to medication and "talk therapy" that is administered at the hospital is electroconvulsive therapy. While antidepressants are effective about 50 percent of the time, electroconvulsive therapy (sometimes known as "shock therapy") is effective 75–90 percent of the time. It is used as a last resort for those suffering various sorts of mental illnesses. ECT consists of administering a small amount of electric shock, lasting only a few seconds, to the brain. Treatments are generally given two or three times per week for several weeks.

While it is stigma-loaded and can affect short-term memory, ECT is usually quite successful. ECT as portrayed in the movies, such as *One Flew over the Cuckoo's Nest* and *A Beautiful Mind* (this was not actually ECT but insulin shock, which is no longer used), does not correspond to the contemporary reality of ECT. In contemporary treatments with ECT, the patient is put to sleep during the procedure, so there is no crying out in pain or fear once the process has started. There are no bodily convulsions; the convulsions are restricted to the brain. Sometimes a toe may wiggle or an eyelash flicker, but that is all.

While it can be terrifying the first few times because it is unfamiliar, it is not the horrendous torture portrayed by Hollywood. In the Hollywood versions, the patient thrashes and screams in agony. This may have been the way ECT was once administered, but now it is much more humane. Even still, patients who have been recommended to take ECT tend to be very wary. I have known people who were terribly depressed and who still pushed away ECT as an option because they were afraid of what it would do to their brain.

The procedure is as follows. First, I am not allowed to eat or drink from midnight until after the ECT treatment. In the morning they bring me down to the treatment room. They do not strap my legs and arms down; thank God for one fewer disgrace. I simply get up onto a regular hospital bed. In the ECT room there are some four beds, with curtains around them that are closed when the procedure itself takes place. The woman on the bed next to me begins to cry out. This is, needless to say, unnerving both to her and to me. Once she gets her anesthesia she will be fine.

> God is our refuge and strength,
>   a very present help in trouble.
> Therefore we will not fear, though the earth be moved,
>   and though the mountains be toppled into the depths
>   of the sea;
> Though its waters rage and foam,
>   and though the mountains tremble at its tumult.
> The Lord of hosts is with us;
>   the God of Jacob is our stronghold.
>
>   Psalm 46:1–4

A nurse inserts an intravenous line into the back of my hand. She prepares the electrodes, which look like metal plates about one and a half inches in diameter with screw holes in the middles. She applies to them something with the consistency and appearance of KY Jelly. Then technicians attach the two electrodes, one to each side of the head, with a large white band that has grommets to attach to the screw holes. The result is that I look like a soldier with a head injury, wrapped in a gauze strap. When they are ready, they insert into the line the anesthesia. For a brief millisecond I can feel it burn from my hand up to and past the underside of my arm. Then, again for a millisecond, which seems much longer, I can sense the anesthesia at the back of my throat, a rubbing alcohol or nail polish odor and taste. Then nothing.

After an hour or so I wake up to the nurse calling me out of my rubbing alcohol/nail polish stupor. Slowly I am able to sit up and am accompanied back to my locked ward. I zigzag to my room and sleep delightfully for another two hours. After that I have a headache. Surprise, surprise. I have just had my head zapped with electricity. Or I may be throwing up upon awakening from the procedure and remain nauseated for the rest of the day because of the anesthesia.

> Bless the LORD, O my soul,
> and all that is within me, bless his holy Name.
> Bless the LORD, O my soul,
> and forget not all his benefits.
> He forgives all your sins
> and heals all your infirmities;
> He redeems your life from the grave
> and crowns you with mercy and loving-kindness.
>
> Psalm 103:1–4

Years later, the hospital has become a not unfamiliar place to me. It no longer carries quite the same threat for me as it once did. Sometimes it has been a refuge, and sometimes a place to rest, but always humbling because I have seen others who suffer as much and even more than I, as though I ever could have thought such a thing was possible. Do not shun hospitalization, if you are ill as was I. It is God's castle to keep us safe. Neither should one shun ECT if it is recommended by a doctor whom you trust. Although I had terrible problems with my memory afterward, I would not hesitate to have ECT if my medications start to fail again. ECT can be an almost immediate lifesaver.

Another type of therapy I was involved in that spring was an outpatient program at the Institute of Living, Hartford Hospital. This was more help than anything except maybe the ECT. Yale Psychiatric Hospital was a safe place for me to be held, a sort of holding tank, until I could get well enough to go back to my life. But the Professionals Program at the Institute of Living used what is called cognitive behavioral therapy (CBT), which meant trying actually to change negative thought patterns: feelings of failure and self-loathing that become habits while one is mentally ill. I spent five weeks in the program. Maybe it was so helpful because I was there for so long.

It was an intensive program for professionals, from teachers and priests to insurance agents and nuns. We spent the hours of 9:00 to 2:00, Monday through Friday, in intensive therapy. They gave us a lot of opportunity for talk therapy. They even had a "gym" program. I have hated gym ever since childhood, and I didn't really like gym at the IOL either, but it was among the most memorable of activities in the program. We were made to play the types of games one plays in youth group: cooperative, noncompetitive games. This meant that we all had to work together on a task or toward a goal. Even participating in these activities, as annoying as they were (who wants to be in youth group again?), was healing. As a team, we could in fact accomplish tasks. We were not, after all, a group of failures.

The companionship there was healing in itself. Even though by this point I could realize that darkness was not in fact my only companion, I still felt mightily alone. No one knew how I was really feeling except my therapist, because I was still trying to hide it—even from my husband. I was still ashamed of my illness. I was still ashamed that I could not rejoice even at the greatest, even at the smallest, of God's gifts. But at IOL, I interacted with people who felt the same way I did: despairing of the future, unable to make decisions, feeling like a complete failure. With others who were religious, in fact: some of the patients were clergy, fathers and sisters. This also meant a lot to me. The loneliness of mental illness only perpetuates the illness, and at the IOL I realized that I was not alone even in my illness.

So it is my opinion that if one is experiencing mental illness, medications and psychiatrists and the hospital and even ECT should not be avoided. It is true that many Christians fear these therapies, as do people in general. I have known people who have been quite frankly deathly ill who still hold these options at bay for fear of them. I will look at this further in chapter 13.

Ultimately, the hospital broke down my impressions of myself as strong. I had to admit that I was weak. This, for the Christian, is an important spiritual lesson that can be learned anywhere, but I happened to learn it under the cover of a place that kept me safe from myself. Being on a locked ward was humiliating. But the Christian knows from her Lord that everyone who exalts herself will be humbled, and everyone who humbles herself will be exalted (Luke 14:11). Maybe I just needed to be humbled that I could know the exaltation of Christ in a new way. But it was a place of healing for me, where Christ entered and pushed back my darkness.

> They will hunger no more, and thirst no more;
>> the sun will not strike them,
>> nor any scorching heat;
> for the Lamb at the center of the throne will be their shepherd,
>> and he will guide them to springs of the water of life,
>> and God will wipe away every tear from their eyes.
>
> Revelation 7:16–17

Part Two

Faith and Mental Illness

7

Feeling, Memory, and Personality

You have given so much to me, give one thing more—a grateful heart.

George Herbert (1593–1633)

Karl Barth, a Swiss theologian of the twentieth century, once said that the creaturely counterpart to the grace of God is gratitude. Is it possible for the depressed soul to be grateful? If not, does this mean that the mentally ill cannot respond to God in creaturely counterpart? What would it look like, what would it mean, for a heart that is cast down to be lifted up in gratitude to God? Sometimes I think the only way for me to be grateful is to pray the psalms. To pray the prayers of Israel. To wrap my tongue around the gracious words of others, in hopes that their words will nourish my soul, somehow sink in and sprout into trees of righteousness, into songs of hope. Because I have no words of gratitude in me, only shame at my absolute hardness of heart.

> Of all the miseries that people experience, sickness is greater than any of them. It is the immediate sword of God. . . . In poverty I lack things and in banishment I lack the company of other people, but in sickness I lack myself.
>
> John Donne (1572–1631)

87

Sometimes the only thing one can do is to hold on to this, that one will once again praise God. "Hope in God; for I shall again prais e him, my help and my God" (Psalm 42:5 NRSV). Hope involves memory, not only of the past but also a "memory" of the future. A promise that the future redemption of Israel will become present in our own lives. This means that memory is such a vitally important part of spiritual health. When one is depressed, memory fills in the gaps that feeling has left vacant. One can't feel God's grace, but one can remember it. There is profound wisdom in the biblical injunction to write the narrative of God's redemption on the doorposts, to talk of it when you sit and when you walk and when you lie down and when you rise: in other words, remind yourself always (Deuteronomy 6:4–9; cf. 11:18-21). In all of the details of life remind yourself of God's redemption, and that memory will be so strong that it will carry you through the times when you can't feel.

This is why it is so important to worship in community, to ask your brothers and sisters in Christ to pray for you, and to pray with them. Sometimes you literally cannot make it on your own, and you need to borrow from the faith of those around you. Sometimes I cannot even recite the creed unless I am doing it in the context of worship, along with all the body of Christ. Now, you could say that this is a faulty memory, and maybe it is in part, but I think it goes further than that. When reciting the creed, I borrow from the recitation of others. Companionship in the Lord Jesus is powerful.

It is like in the story of the paralytic in Mark 2: His friends are determined to have Jesus heal him, so they rip apart the roof and let him in on his pallet down to Jesus. "When Jesus saw *their* faith, he said to the paralytic, 'Son, your sins are forgiven.'" The faith of the friends is crucial for the paralytic's healing. I have borrowed from the faithfulness of the community, the body of Christ, and I believe that the faith of my community has been crucial for my own healing. One blessing that we can hope to wrestle out of God in this Jacob-like struggle is that we may at daybreak finally learn what grace really is.

Depression and madness? I think I am coming to see that when most people talk about depression we are not talking about the same thing. And it is so hard to talk about. I am not talking about down-in-the-dumps-grumps. That is not madness, I agree.

But when major depression gets truly bad, it is indeed like madness. The personality dissolves. Tastes, desires, dispositions that formerly marked our personality vanish with mental illness. Will I ever be me again, and if so, what will me be on the other side of this madness? So what does this mean? What does this mean *coram Deo*, before God, that the personality should dissolve? I suppose it means that the personality is relatively unimportant vis-à-vis God. In God's eyes we are not how we feel, we are not what we think, we are not even what we do. We are what God does with us, and what God does with us is to save us from our best yet perverse efforts to separate ourselves from his presence, from his fellowship, communion, sharing.

Of course, saying that the personality is not very important is not stylish these days, to say the least. I think many people think of God as a self-help device, to improve our personality: to help us quit smoking, drinking, overeating, abusing our kids. To help us be nicer people, so we can stand to live in our own skin, to help us have more friends. To say that God doesn't really care too much about our personality is to deny that God is deeply concerned about these things. Personality and its betterment motivates much religion in America these days, because most of us are functional atheists, even though we may be quite pious indeed. We can't imagine how our religion would require anything of us that would not be directed solely to our own betterment. But if God is really the God of the Bible, then that God demands our worship and obedience despite how we feel about it, despite how we feel about ourselves or about others. Of course, it would be nice to feel good. And it would be especially nice not to go through life wanting to end it. But even this doesn't separate us from God. Even wanting to return the gift of life does not damn us. "God proves his love for us in that while we were still sinners, Christ died for us" (Romans 5:8). Even before we made the slightest move out of our sloth to reach out to God. The hard part is choosing life, though, and it is ever demanded of us. That is the hard part. How we feel does not change anything objectively about our life before God.

What will allow for our survival is not how we feel but what we remember. The Baal Shem-Tov (1698–1760, founder of the Hasidic movement) once said, "Exile is caused by forgetfulness, and the secret of redemption is memory." I must remember, even if I don't feel it, that I am part of a people of faith, of hope, of love. I cannot doubt or question that memory, even though all evidence would lead me to conclude that I never really did trust, never really did hope, never really did love. I may feel like a hypocrite now for even pretending to pray. But how I feel, after all, is not that important. If I can do nothing else, I must simply remember that I am a part of the community of faith, the body of Christ, that I was once able to participate in the praises of Israel. "Put your trust in God; for I will yet give thanks to him, who is the help of my countenance, and my God" (Psalm 42:5). That will sustain us, and it may be all that sustains us. Remembering the past anchors hope for the future. It may not change how we feel, but it will help us to endure.

> Hear O Israel: The LORD is our God, the LORD alone. You shall love the LORD your God with all your heart, and with all your soul, and with all your might. Keep these words that I am commanding you today in your heart. Recite them to your children and talk about them when you are at home and when you are away, when you lie down and when you rise.
>
> Deuteronomy 6:4

Thus has Israel remembered the glories of her God, his gifts, his mercies, his leading. She remembers the past and thereby allows God to build a future with her. Without the memories of God's past with Israel, Israel has no reason for present strength or future hope.

If it is true that memory of the past serves not so much to preserve the past as to create a present for us and to reach out to the future, what does it mean when we are not able to remember? What of the person who physically can no longer remember? Think of the disadvantage to the soul. David Keck writes of his mother's illness with Alzheimer's syndrome in his book *Forgetting Whose We Are*. This is exactly the tragedy: we cannot remember and thus we lose track of whose we are. Objectively of course our identity in Christ remains the same, but forgetfulness deprives our consciousness of great solace. The great tragedy of this is the break in relationships: here again, past affects present and future.

So my own memories should give me hope. The New Testament memories of the resurrection of Jesus should give me a past, present, and future; just as we proclaim the mystery of faith in our liturgy, "Christ has died, Christ is risen, Christ will come again." God's past faithfulness to me should undergird and shield me from my despair. Does it? Only when I am able to absorb these acts of faithful care into my memory. But sometimes my memory is compromised by the medication, the ECT, and the depression. With hope this will get better soon.

After the ECT, I was unable to remember much at all. I could not remember my bank codes, my own phone number, the kind of car I drove. This made finding it in a parking lot doubly difficult; not only did I forget where I had left it, I forgot what it was that I had left. I forgot the details of the books I had written, even the outline of the history of Israel and the New Testament. It was so bad that I had to cancel speaking engagements, and in a job interview I so thoroughly forgot even my dissertation that I made a complete fool of myself. Needless to say, I did not get that job. I am sure the interviewers thought I was a lame case, overrated by my professors.

I also had to have an IQ test in preparation for being ordained to the priesthood in the Episcopal Church, and the psychologist examining me proclaimed my IQ to be 93. Never mind that I have three graduate degrees from Yale University. I simply could not fathom how to put a set of blocks together to make the indicated shapes. I could not remember from second to second what I was doing, nor could I discern each future step in the process. My shame at that event was surpassed only by the psychologist's telling me later that I would not be passed on to the bishop with recommendation for ordination. I thank God for my bishop's understanding and willingness to look beyond the obvious. He, at least, understood that mental illness is just that: an illness that with the proper care one can overcome, even if never completely "cured."

Throughout the Bible we see the importance of memory, of memorizing, of remembering. "My soul is heavy within me; therefore I will remember you from the land of Jordan, and from the peak of Mizar among the heights of Hermon" (Psalm 42:8). The heaviness of the soul ("Why are you so full of heaviness, O my soul? and why are you so disquieted within me?" [Psalm 42:6]) in particular is counteracted by remembrance of concrete places and acts God has done. Memory of God's mercies begets healing of the soul from heaviness to thanksgiving, the biblical model of health.

The same is true of form in the liturgy: we can memorize the prayers, the collects, the creed, so they come back to us throughout the week to nourish our soul. But even that is denied someone whose memory is compromised. I would reach for the words of collects and prayers and be left with a blank. For people with intact memory, the forms of the liturgy themselves are like memories that reach to the past, establish the present, and secure hope in the future. Denominations that do not have a prayer book are unfortunately lacking in this respect. Their hymnals sometimes serve this purpose, but since these congregations tend to make up their forms every week, the worshipers rarely come to internalize in memory in the same way. It is like the difference between J. S. Bach and John Cage: the former used existing forms and composed broadly, while the latter had to invent the forms himself and left fewer than one-tenth of Bach's number of compositions. The liturgy sinks into our soul and can come back in time of need in its forms through our memory.

Ironically, forgetfulness is all one wants when profoundly depressed. In a manic state, before it turns sour, one is so elated as not to think about memory. Who cares about anything but the present in mania? This is part of the problem. But depressed, one wants simply to be unaware of the present, to forget all cause and reason for depression. What is good for a healthy person and for the sick is despised by the sick. This is an example of the perversity of mental illness. The thing that could aid in healing is often shunned by the mentally ill, and forms of self-destruction are sometimes sought.

As a deer longs for the water-brooks,
    so longs my soul for you, O God.
My soul is athirst for God, athirst for the living God.
    when shall I come to appear before the presence of God?
My tears have been my food day and night,
    while all day they say to me,
    "Where now is your God?"
I pour out my soul when I think on these things:
    how I went with the multitude and led them into the house
        of God,
With the voice of praise and thanksgiving,
    among those who keep holy-day.
Why are you so full of heaviness, O my soul?
    and why are you so disquieted within me?

Put your trust in God;
   for I will yet give thanks to him,
   who is the help of my countenance, and my God.

Psalm 42:1–7

In the midst of an impenetrable depression, one is often unable to sense the presence of God at all. Sometimes all one can feel is the complete absence of God, one's utter abandonment by God, the ridiculousness of the very notion of a loving and merciful God. This cuts to the heart of the Christian and challenges everything she believes about the world and about herself. But if one is depressed, one should not expect to feel otherwise. In fact, feeling is not really that important for the life of faith.

Ever since Friedrich Schleiermacher's (1768–1834) definition of religion as the feeling of absolute dependence, people in the Protestant West have tended to define religion in terms of feeling or experience. Once G. W. F. Hegel (1770–1831) quipped that if Christianity were the feeling of absolute dependence, his dog would be the best Christian ever. If we really believed that feeling is the essence of the Christian faith, the depressed Christian would be given all the more ammunition for self-destruction. Since she cannot by definition feel anything but violence toward and hatred of the self, if that "feeling" were to be validated as religiously significant, then the tendency toward self-annihilation would only be fueled. Often we simply cannot change the way we feel. Despair, abandonment, isolation, and meaninglessness are sometimes unavoidable, and sheer endurance is the only way to deal with them. It is a good thing, then, that God does not look upon us according to our feelings but according to the faithfulness of Jesus Christ.

Of course, feelings and their examination are key in the work of psychotherapy. I am not denying the importance of being honest with one's feelings in psychotherapy for health of mind, and maybe even soul. I am simply questioning the religious significance of feelings, especially for the Christian religion, in the economy of salvation. Our salvation is something Jesus wrought on the cross, not in the interiority of our personality. When our personality dissolves with mental illness, this does not mean that God regards our soul any differently from when we are mentally healthy.

8

Brain, Mind, and Soul

The soul that to Jesus hath fled for repose,
I will not, I will not desert to its foes;
That soul, though all hell should endeavor to shake,
I'll never, no never, no never forsake.

John Rippon (1751–1836)

According to the Smithsonian, your brain makes up only 2 percent of your body's weight but uses 20 percent of your body's fuel. Such a miracle. But my "enemy," in the psalmist's terms, has been my brain itself. The gray matter inside my skull. The physical organ without which I could not live, without which I would have no functioning mind. The mind seems to be more abstract than the brain, serving more as intellect in the relation between the brain and the world of ideas and social interaction. It is the mind that may or may not apprehend God as an intellectual idea or problem.

What is, then, the relation between the brain and the soul? Is it similar to the relation between the brain and the mind? Does the soul equal the mind, as the capacity for consciousness and memory? If the brain is the biological organ itself, and the mind is the seat of consciousness, memory, and the social, the soul might be seen as the whole person, the self, through which we have communion with God. While it may take the mind to apprehend God as a problem, it takes the soul to apprehend God as Holy Trinity and to love God.

Of course, seeing these as three distinct items—brain, mind, and soul—even if inseparable, is not the usual view of much of philosophy. Some think that the mind is merely the functioning brain, and the soul, if it is spoken of at all, is merely the mind. If under this line of thought the brain is like the constructed TV set and the mind is like the working of the TV set, what is the soul in this view?

I am not interested here in the ancient question and its traditional answers regarding the relation between the soul and the body. It is clear from biblical teaching, especially from the Old Testament, that the soul and body are united, however we choose to talk about that. Certainly the resurrection body is different from our earthly body (1 Corinthians 15:35–55). The doctrine of the resurrection of the body requires this. The words at the distribution of the sacrament, "The body of our Lord Jesus Christ, given for you, preserve your *body and soul* unto everlasting life," also assume the unity of body and soul.

I am also not terribly invested here in the question of what happens to the soul after death. Since it is in the image of the triune God, we can be comforted that God will hold the soul of the Christian, whether we think that the soul "sleeps" after death unto the general resurrection, or that the soul immediately is taken after death to God, or that eternal life starts here and now. Nor am I interested, here, in the question of the creation of the soul.

I am more interested at the moment in the specific relation between the brain, the mind, and the soul in mental illness. One could say that the same questions arise in relation to any kind of physical suffering, and while that may be true, in the suffering of mental illness the brain and mind play a unique role. I want to suggest that while it is true that the brain of a mentally ill person is in fact ill, the soul is not necessarily so.

After I had my first round of ECT, I underwent an MRI (magnetic resonance imaging) of my brain. I was given a mild anesthetic and then trundled into a coffinlike tube, where I had to remain very still for far too long while the machine whirred and clanked around me. The ECT treatments had left me so disoriented that the doctor wanted to make sure there was nothing anatomically wrong with my brain, such as a tumor. I was fine, of course—or rather, I was in an agony of confusion but had no tumor. I have heard since then that a PET (positron emission tomography) scan can tell by the colors of the different parts of the brain whether or not a patient is depressed. A PET scan is a very expensive way to discover this, though, when a litany of straightforward questions could render the same diagnosis. ("Are you depressed?" The science of psychiatry is sometimes very elementary.) Still, the fact that metabolically the depressed brain takes on different colors in a PET scan, even if the brain is anatomically healthy, is fascinating to me. We can say, then, incorporating the medical model, that depression is a physical event with spiritual side effects. Yet even according to the medical model, the physical illness of depression can be brought on by what are called "psychological" events or stressors, or what the Christian may sometimes see as spiritual events.

The redeemed soul longs for God. This is part of its function: to reach out to its Creator and to seek and be sought by God. The fallen soul naturally longs for created things, not the Creator. The Christian, caught between these two longings in the now-and-not-yet of the Christian "time zone," longs for both God and for God's creation. Depression may intensify this longing of the soul for God, since it makes the created order so despicable. Thus depression can be a good in and of itself, when the soul's thirst for God is increased (as it was in my case).

Since only God is the source of all healing, it is appropriate that the Christian soul sometimes searches for God more in depression than in health. But the soul reaches out and often cannot find. Depression increases our longing for the Healing One yet veils our view of him. "We were made for Thee and our hearts are restless until they rest in Thee" (Augustine, 354–430). The jewels of the world never fill the soul—and in mental illness, for the Christian, this is more agonizingly the case. Nothing in the world satisfies, but the longing is intensified. All becomes a seeking for God, for God's blessing and God's comfort. Yet even while this longing is intensified, its goal is painfully removed from view. The soul thirsts for God and yet is pushed further away from the source of its slaking.

> The whole round world is not enough to fill
> The heart's three corners, but it craveth still:
> None but the Trinity, who made it, can
> Suffice the vast triangulated heart of man.
>
> Christopher Harvey (1597–1663)

Adam is created from the dust, and God breathes into his nostrils the breath of life, and the man becomes a "living being" (*nephesh hayah*: living soul). He does not have a soul; he *is* soul, an ensouled body and an embodied soul. Along with the body, the soul is the totality of the human creature, brain, mind, feelings, actions, inclinations, desires, and life. All of these aspects affect the soul, but they do not add up to the soul. Since God is the One who shapes the soul, calls it, imprints it with his image, and sends it out as witness to his grace in the world, the soul cannot be simply a collection of the functions of the human mind. Since the triune God is himself being-in-relation, to be ensouled body means to be created in the image of this God, and also means to be in relation to all creation.

Mental illness breaks this continuum of relationship, since the sufferer is rendered virtually unable to relate. Mental illness threatens to turn us in upon ourselves. It does not necessarily destroy the relational continuum, unless the sufferer should commit the final act of negation of all relation, suicide.

Mental illness can potentially damage the soul, since it preys on the brain and the mind, but it cannot *destroy* the soul, for God holds the soul in his hands. "Do not fear those who kill the body but cannot kill the soul; rather fear him who can destroy both soul and body in hell" (Matt. 10:28). God is the only One who has the power to destroy both body and soul. What does this mean for suicides who destroy their own body? The Christian's relation with the triune God may not stop with suicide. Even though suicide is clearly an ultimate separation from fellow creatures, it is not more so than natural death. And natural death does not stop God from loving the soul, or the soul from loving God.

Eternal and most glorious God, you have stamped the soul of
humanity with your Image, received it into your revenue, and
made it part of your treasure; do not allow us so to undervalue
ourselves, so to impoverish you, as to give away these souls for
nothing, and all the world is nothing if the soul must be given for
it. Do this, O God, for his sake who knows our natural infirmities,
for he had them, and knows the weight of our sins, for he paid a
dear price for them; your Son, our Savior Jesus Christ.

John Donne (1572–1631)

This has implications for how the church treats suicides. If I
am right and suicide does not destroy the soul of the Christian,
then why would any church have difficulties burying suicides
or comforting the families left behind? A baptized Christian remains a Christian. Possibly the difficulty lies in the horror and
shame of the suicide. She is outcast in death because she could
not live, because she was not able to go on living. It is perceived
as a failure on the part of the suicide, the family, and the church.
Further, suicide is a transgression of the commandment not to
kill. To live is an act of obedience to God.

What does this mean for my own illness? Most of the time
when I was ill, I was unable consciously to witness to the grace
of God. Or at least so I felt. Even then my sermons were still
greeted with appreciation by my parish. But I have already ques-
tioned the value of feeling in religion. If my feelings were dead
vis-à-vis God, this does not mean that my soul was sick. My brain
certainly was sick, and my mind was sick, but God held my soul
firmly throughout, keeping me longing for him—even though it
felt as if I had been abandoned. Abandonment, however, is not
God's way of operating.

Is the soul different then from the heart or the spirit? These
latter words are both biblical terms that are used in tandem with
soul. "You shall love the Lord your God with all your heart, and
with all your soul, and with all your strength, and with all your
mind, and your neighbor as yourself" (Luke 10:27; cf. Leviticus
19:18; Deuteronomy 6:5). *Heart*, *soul*, and *mind* are not three
distinct faculties but different biblical terms that designate the
very being of the person.

Another way of looking at the soul, from one purely scientific
view, is that we are all animal and the "soul" is simply the brain.

In this view, our personhood can be seen in consciousness, love, friendship, and morality.[1] But we are basically all animal, since the soul itself would be equated with the brain. Certainly the Christian tradition does agree that humanity is animal, and created as such, but it teaches that human beings were created good by God and made a living soul. And God reckons that creation of humanity is "very good" over and above all the other animals and works of creation (Genesis 1:31).

Another way of looking at the soul is to let it answer the question of the central "whatness" of humanity, the way René Descartes's "I think, therefore I am" functioned to answer the "whatness" with rationality. What about the human whatness can be said in reference to the mentally ill? When I was mentally ill, self-reflective thinking itself was terribly difficult. At times it was impossible. Shall I then say that "I was not"? It certainly felt that way, but I understand feelings, as I have said, to be untrustworthy in one's relationship to God. Maybe an affirmation more central to the whatness of humanity would be "I love, therefore I am," since according to scripture love brings us into the very ground of our being, God. The objective nature of God's love for me was what brought me through the darkness and kept me from giving up on myself and all those around me.

But the mentally ill sometimes cannot love aright. Consider the mother in Texas who on November 24, 2004, severed the arms from her eight-month-old daughter, killing her. A mother is supposed to love and protect her child. What then of this woman's humanity, of her soul? Due to God's love for her it could have still been active and healthy, even though the brain and mind were desperately sickened. Her own love for God is compromised by her actions and her mental life, but it is God alone who can make the final call about this woman's soul.

What makes the soul and therefore the human is God's love, not the soul's love for anything else. Therefore we might best say that the "whatness" of humanity is "I *am loved*, therefore I am." This is in part what the Christian tradition means by the

---

1. Owen Flanagan, *The Problem of the Soul: Two Visions of Mind and How to Reconcile Them* (New York: Basic Books, 2002), xv. Another book that came out too late for me to use but that looks promising to the discussion is Joel B. Green and Stuart Palmer, eds., *In Search of the Soul: Four Views of the Mind-Body Problem* (Downers Grove, IL: InterVarsity Press, 2005).

creation of humanity by God. The soul is loved into existence by God.

What is the relation between our consciousness, feelings, thoughts, desires—that is, our mental life—and our brain and our soul? First of all, we see by the mere existence of feelings, thoughts, and desires that our mind is more than just a brain. The brain is the physical organ that allows the function of the mind, and of the body for that matter. Because the image of God is in us, we can see that the soul is more than both of these combined. The soul is not the sum of the parts of the nonphysical, because it is created by God and sustained by God; this gives the soul an objectivity beyond the merely nonphysical aspects of "me."

Notice what I am *not* saying. One philosopher compares the soul to a light bulb and the brain to the socket into which the soul is "plugged." The soul will "function (have a mental life) if it is plugged into a functioning brain."[2] The implication is that the soul's function is to have a mental life. If that were so, mentally ill people would have sick souls, since their mental life is indeed compromised, but this is not consistent with a biblical understanding of the soul. I have said that the function of the soul is to witness to the image of God and to reach out for God in praise and thanksgiving. Instead of the light bulb analogy, whereby the sick soul is associated with a sick brain, I would suggest that the sick soul is the soul of the person who does not witness to the image of God in herself to her world. This may have something to do with mental illness, but more likely it does not. It may have to do with despising Christianity, or simply not knowing enough about it to understand what witness to the image of God would mean. It is those who do not return thanks to God who are soul-sick, not necessarily the mentally ill.

What then does all of this mean for the mentally ill? When, as in mental illness, love, friendship, even morality in cases of suicidality from depression or hypersexuality in mania are all brought into question, does this mean that the soul itself is in question? For the Christian tradition, meaningful life is not based on our human desires or our consciousness but solely in our relationship to the God of Israel, the triune God who endows

2. Richard Swinburne, *The Evolution of the Soul* (Oxford: Oxford University Press/Clarendon, 1986), 310.

our lives with meaning. The soul is not the seat of sickness in the mentally ill; it is the brain, its synapses and receptors and so on, that renders the mind broken. The soul, as the self in relation to God, continues healthy in anyone as long as that person is in Christ, relating to and witnessing to God.

> The soul that to Jesus has fled for repose
> I will not, I will not desert to its foes. . . .

9

Sin, Suffering, and Despair

Lord God, almighty and everlasting Father, you have brought us in safety to this new day: Preserve us with your mighty power, that we may not fall into sin, nor be overcome by adversity; and in all that we do, direct us to the fulfilling of your purpose, through Jesus Christ our Lord. Amen.

BCP, 137

What is the relationship between suffering in mental illness and sin? Is mental illness caused by sin, or is it in some way a punishment for sin? On the one hand I would say no, that does not sound worthy of God. And yet of course we suffer because of our sins of commission and omission all the time. The psalmist says:

> There is no health in my flesh
> because of your indignation;
>   there is no soundness in my body, because of my sin.
> For my iniquities overwhelm me;
>   like a heavy burden they are too much for me to bear.

Psalm 38:3–4

How can this be so? Is it really true that I am sick because of my
misdeeds toward God and neighbor? Like a heavy burden, this
thought is too much for me to bear. Here is an example, from
the prayer book of Israel, of what mental illness can feel like
when God's wrath is the cause[1]:

> LORD, do not rebuke me in your anger;
>   do not punish me in your wrath.
> Have pity on me, LORD, for I am weak;
>   heal me, LORD, for my bones are racked.
> My spirit shakes with terror;
>   how long, O LORD, how long?
> Turn, O LORD, and deliver me;
>   save me for your mercy's sake.
> For in death no one remembers you;
>   and who will give you thanks in the grave?
> I grow weary because of my moaning;
>   every night I drench my bed
>   and flood my couch with tears.
> My eyes are wasted away with grief
>   and worn because of all my enemies.
> Depart from me, all evildoers,
>   for the LORD has heard the sound of my weeping.
> The LORD has heard my supplication;
>   the LORD accepts my prayer.
> All my enemies shall be confounded and quake with fear;
>   they shall turn back and suddenly be put to shame.
>
>   Psalm 6

Here the psalmist understands his own suffering as a symptom
of the anger of God. How unpopular such an understanding of
the wrath of God is in our culture. We prefer to see God as nice,
indeed rather innocuous. To blame illness on the anger of God is
to lay upon God perhaps too much power, too much stridency and
wrath for the broader cultural understanding of God. But notice
that these words in a sense comfort the psalmist: "LORD, do not
rebuke me in your anger!" The psalmist is allowed to ask for God's

---

1. This is not to say that the psalmist was "mentally ill," a category that certainly would be only anachronistically applied here, but rather that the mentally
ill can identify with the suffering of the psalmist. The psalms of lament all testify
to suffering and faithfulness before God.

mercy. At least we know that there is a cause of the suffering. It is not random or ill-placed. It is because of God's anger. This is not so, for example, for William Styron: "The pain is unrelenting, and what makes the condition intolerable is the foreknowledge that no remedy will come—not in a day, an hour, a month, or a minute." Styron's suffering is meaningless, whereas the psalmist is drawn into relationship with God in his suffering.

And there is a way out of this situation for the psalmist, while there is no way out of random suffering: "Do not punish me in your wrath!" God listens to the prayers of his people and takes pity. Otherwise there would be no point for the psalmist to make a plea: "Have pity on me, LORD, for I am weak!" The psalmist even pleads with God, making a deal: you must not let me die, because if you did you would only have one fewer to praise you! At the end of the psalm, the LORD has heard the prayer of the psalmist, and the psalmist gloats over his enemies who will be confounded. It would not be inappropriate to read the enemies here as the symptoms a mentally ill person might have. These symptoms are certainly enemies, and they shall be turned back, according to the psalm. The psalmist's cry turns to a shout of joy and hope, not because of any inner reflection or reasoning but because "the LORD has heard the sound of my weeping."

Notice how different the psalm is from the descriptions of mental illness by modern authors. The psalmist cries out in pain ("I . . . flood my couch with tears") and exhibits symptoms ("my eyes are wasted with grief"). But a psalm is more than just a lament: it founds its lament and its trust on the faithfulness of God to bring healing. Can we not understand healing to come from God in the way the psalmist says ("the LORD accepts my prayer")?

> When evening had come, he said to them, "Let us go across to the other side." And leaving the crowd behind, they took him with them in the boat, just as he was. Other boats were with him. A great windstorm arose, and the waves beat into the boat, so that the boat was already being swamped. But he was in the stern, asleep on the cushion; and they woke him up and said to him, "Teacher, do you not care that we are perishing?"
>
> Mark 4:35–38

Teacher, do you not care that I am perishing? Do you not see that
the waves are already overtaking my boat? Do you sleep? The
One who watches over Israel shall neither slumber nor sleep:
are you really that Good Shepherd?

> He woke up and rebuked the wind, and said to the sea, "Peace! Be
> still!" Then the wind ceased, and there was a dead calm. He said
> to them, "Why are you afraid? Have you still no faith?" And they
> were filled with great awe and said to one another, "Who then is
> this, that even the wind and the sea obey him?"
>
> Mark 4:39–41

Rebuke the wind, calm the waves, still the chaos within. You
who were present at the creation of the world, within the very
bosom of God the Father, you who at creation calmed the stormy
chaos of the waters by creating the land, the dry land on which
humanity is to live, protected from the waters of destruction,
dear Word of God, in me create islands of peace, footholds in
the midst of the raging sea.

Grant, dear Lord, that I may again be of use to you, to teach
your Law and your Grace. Clear my thoughts, calm my thinking,
dwell in my heart as its only Teacher and Guide.

> They came to the other side of the sea, to the country of the
> Gerasenes. And when he had stepped out of the boat, immedi-
> ately a man out of the tombs with an unclean spirit met him.
> He lived among the tombs; and no one could restrain him any
> more, even with a chain; for he had often been restrained with
> shackles and chains, but the chains he wrenched apart, and
> the shackles he broke in pieces; and no one had the strength
> to subdue him. Night and day among the tombs and on the
> mountains he was always howling and bruising himself with
> stones. When he saw Jesus from a distance, he ran and bowed
> down before him; and he shouted at the top of his voice, "What
> have you to do with me, Jesus, Son of the Most High God? I
> adjure you by God, do not torment me." For he had said to him,
> "Come out of the man, you unclean spirit!" Then Jesus asked
> him, "What is your name?" He replied, "My name is Legion;
> for we are many." He begged him earnestly not to send them
> out of the country.
>
> Mark 5:1–10

We are legion. But we are usually invisible to the naked eye. We look as if we are a human being, when the human being is in fact merely the host for our banquet, our silent devouring of flesh and guzzling of blood. Parasitic. We make our hosts walk among the living as though dead, and most of the time the living cannot recognize that we are survivors within the dying host.

Until we make our host so sick that she would choose tombs for a dwelling. Until we make our host so sick that she needs to be bound by chains. And especially when even the chains cannot bind our host, the living see just how much we have sucked the life out of her. But sometimes all they see is the host, and they blame the host, as if she had choice in the matter of having demons suck the life out of her. So the living are often just as happy to slough off the host to dwell among the tombs. To shunt the impurity away from the dwellings of the seemingly pure.

At such a point, it is Jesus who has the power to bind our diseases, for he is the Strong Man. He knows that our disease, our demons, are separate from ourselves. To the depressed, the disease seems to take over, until one is entirely an illness. Jesus knows this is not true, and he can cast out the demons without destroying us. Only he can cast out of us our impurity, our uncleanness. Demons from the host among the tombs into the pigs, then into the sea. Impurity dwelling among the impure is cast into the impure and then herded into the chaos.

The thing is that the man's demons don't want to go away, don't want to be cast out. It is easier to dwell where you are than to allow Jesus to rout you out, even if where you are is the cemetery, living among the walking dead.

> Blessed be the God and Father of our Lord Jesus Christ! By his great mercy he has given us a new birth into a living hope through the resurrection of Jesus Christ from the dead.
>
> 1 Peter 1:3

This story about the demoniac living among the tombs functions somewhat like the passion predictions later in Mark 8:30, 9:30, and 10:33–34. But here the passion is illustrated rather than stated, in the form of a miracle story, somewhat like the story of the raising of Lazarus in John's Gospel. Here Jesus conquers the legion of demons, clothing the man in his right mind, giving him new life, and restoring him to community among the living.

And how this disturbs the swineherds. Resurrection sticks in the throat, not only for the demons but for all who deal with and pander in impurity.

We await the day when we may regain the peace of Adam and Eve, who were "naked and not ashamed," when we will be fully clothed in the power of the resurrection. *By his great mercy he has given us a new birth into a living hope through the resurrection of Jesus Christ from the dead* (1 Peter 1:3).

To speak of the mentally ill and demons in the same breath can be truly offensive to those with brain disorders that are called mental illnesses—especially if mental illness is *equated with* demon possession and vice versa. Mental illnesses are understood these days as biologically and socially based, not spiritually. But they do have spiritual fallout. And the Christian knows that the Strong Man who will bind this spiritual fallout is Jesus. For this we who live among so many tombs do have hope. But we have to remember that. And we have to pray, although that may seem impossible while we are in a mental illness.

> The Lord's arm is not too short to save, nor his ear too dull to hear. Rather, your iniquities have been barriers between you and your God, and your sins have hidden his face from you so that he does not hear.
>
> Isaiah 59:1–2

This is a hard saying. It is my iniquities that raise a barrier between me and God? Because of my sins God hides his face from me? Now this would never go over well with my psychiatrist. Any relation of my illness and guilt before God would be quickly swept away at best, and openly confronted at worst. But how am I to read this? Yes, of course, it was the chosen people's iniquities that caused God in Isaiah's time to turn a deaf ear. What sins have I that God would turn his face from me? How are my sins any different from most people's, that I would be stuck with this awful disease? My doctors and therapists would never want me to say this bipolar disorder is my fault. Neither would I. But Isaiah and other writers throughout the Bible link suffering and disaster with sin.

The challenge is placed for me therefore to look to my own heart and see if this is the case for me. Maybe my doctors would look at the question this way: to what extent do your desires and fears and activities trip you up so as to let mental illness gain a foothold? Maybe where they would say desires, I would say misplaced desires; where they would say fears, I would say faithless fears; where they say activities, I would say disobedient acts. But they would probably not even go this far. They would say that mental illness is a biological problem exacerbated by stress in one's life. And I believe that, so far as it goes.

But I as a Christian must struggle with the question of sin. How does my disobedience to God cause me to suffer? More important, how does the Christian understand sin? My sin is manifest in my many little misdeeds, and even big ones, but the power that separates us from God is the greater understanding of sin. This power makes us commit our little and large acts of disobedience and omit obedience. This power, like a force field, is overcome in the power of the cross and resurrection, whose force field is greater than that of sin.

> LORD, be merciful to me;
> heal me, for I have sinned against you.
>
> Psalm 41:4

Then again, in John 9, at the healing of the man born blind, it is the disciples themselves who ask, "Rabbi, who sinned, this man or his parents, that he was born blind?" Jesus answered that neither the man born blind nor his parents had sinned, but rather he was born blind so that God's works might be revealed in him. Can this illness in me show God's works? That would make it all worth it to me. As G. K. Chesterton (1874–1936) once said, "One sees great things from the valley, only small things from the peak." Perhaps God has thrust me into this valley that I might see his mountain from the underside.

From the valley of depression one does see more than from the peaks of mania, or even the peaks of "normal" happiness. Why does my illness give me wisdom? Do I want this kind of wisdom, born of so much suffering?

Surely he has borne our griefs and carried our sorrows;
yet we esteemed him stricken, smitten by God, and afflicted.
But he was wounded for our transgressions,
he was bruised for our iniquities;
upon him was the chastisement that made us whole,
and with his stripes we are healed.
All we like sheep have gone astray,
we have turned every one to his own way;
and the LORD has laid on him the iniquity of us all.

Isaiah 53:4–6 (RSV)

Does the LORD lay on Jesus the iniquity of us all? Can I say that my sins are borne away in the shadow of his wings? Why then do I continue to suffer? Have I just turned astray, like the lost sheep? Is this all my fault?

As a door turns on its hinges, so does a sluggard on his bed.

Prov. 26:14 (RSV)

Am I a sluggard then? Is my disease making me a sinner? I find it hard to believe that a biological deficit in my brain could make me more of a sinner than I already am. But, depressed, I cannot even turn on my bed. I lie motionless, on my left side. It was on my left side that I was told to lie when I had preterm labor with both of my children. I hated lying still then; I felt caged. I was a human incubator, with no other function than to reach full term, which lay weeks ahead. But, depressed, I don't even mark the time. I sigh. I lie still, staring off into space, content to be caged within my brain. *Content?* No, such a word cannot be applied to a depressive.

Accidie. Often translated as sloth. Is despair, as sloth, actually a sin? Is it actually like pride, murder, covetousness, lust, envy, gluttony, and anger? Of course there are sins that can come of the sin of despair, and maybe I am just too Protestant to speak of the deadly or mortal sins, but how can a physical disease be considered a sin? How can the fact of sloth caused by depression be considered in itself a sin? Yes, it may be a symptom of the power of Sin, but to call it an individual sin is more than it can bear. The depressed may be slothful or may not be. The slothful may be depressed, but they are not necessarily so.

John Cassian (360–435) understood accidie to be a state of restlessness and inability to work or pray. It is supposed to affect monks and hermits particulary, who live mostly in seclusion. Of course, I always found seclusion to be poisonous to me when depressed. Assiduous prayer is prescribed by Cassian as the remedy for accidie.

Now, do I have accidie? Even though I am no monk, I suppose that I could be exhibiting accidie. But is accidie depression or some form of mental illness? No, I would say clearly not. Many depressed people are slothful, yet this isn't the mark of depression for me nor for my friends who are mothers. When you are a mother, you can never let go of your basic tasks except for brief times. Intense pain while still engaging in the tasks of the day may be the mother's mark of depression. Most mothers, indeed, do not have the luxury of putting off the needs and desires of their children. If a mother is very ill, caretakers for the children will be necessary unless the husband is able not to work. Postpartum depression can be very dangerous if no one is available to help support the mother.

I have known very active people who were very depressed. While many depressed people may be slothful, the one who is slothful may just be self-indulgent. This is one of the keys to the stigma of mental illness: other people think that the mentally ill are just being self-indulgent. This may be true, but it often is not true of the one who is truly mentally ill.

Every time we can check despair and by the grace of God push it away and keep it from entering into our actions, God is glorified. But we must learn why it is we feel whatever it is we are feeling. This may take a long time, and patience and endurance may be required. We must push the despair away and keep it from entering our actions insofar as we are able, while keeping the despair in mind enough to acknowledge it and maybe even to understand it. This is painful, it is not easy, but it may be a part of what God requires in this testing. And someday God may use us to help others facing a similar test.

Ultimately, though, I think the despair of mental illness itself has no meaning. If it did, that meaning would be of God, because all meaning is of God. Any coherence in the midst of chaos, any sense in the midst of nonsense, is the work of God. If the despair had meaning, if there were in fact a purpose or reason for it, it would not be despair but something else. Mental illness is the lack of meaning, just as evil is the lack or privation of the good.

This is again one of the places where the theologian and the classical psychotherapist part. I cannot say: *This* is the only the reason I feel this way—this psychological scar, that chemical deficiency, this trauma, that breakdown in the personality. These may be good explanations on the psychobiological level, but they do not point to any ultimate meaning, any theological reality. Insofar as despair has a theological reality, it is evil. It is the absence (so present you can feel it, taste it, sometimes even, heaven forbid, see it and hear it) of the good. It is a black hole, a void, an emptiness. But we need to remember that God is the One who calls order out of chaos, who called the land to separate the waters (Genesis 1:9), who called created order out of the formlessness and void. And God calls even us into creation, out of nothingness into life before him.

> "Woman, why are you weeping?" She said to them, "They have taken away my Lord, and I do not know where they have laid him."
>
> John 20:13

I thought I knew who Jesus was. I thought I could sense his presence. But in mental illness, I weep like Mary, "They have taken away my Lord, and I do not know where they have laid him." My presuppositions about the love of the Lord have been turned upside down. My brain, my cognition and my memory, can't find Jesus. Only my soul itself is safe in the Lord, without my awareness.

Sin, suffering, and despair are thus linked in mental illness, yet not in a straightforward one-to-one correspondence. The mentally ill, just like anyone else, may be suffering on account of the power of sin in the world; indeed all suffering can be seen in this way. When I was sick I needed to see God's presence even in this way, even in my suffering, even *because of* the power of sin. If I hadn't seen God in this way, as punishing my sin, as eradicating the force of sin in the world, then my suspicions would have been confirmed: that darkness was in fact my only companion and that God had indeed abandoned me.

IO

Dark Night, Discipline, and the Hiddenness of God

Darkness is not dark to you;
the night is as bright as the day;
darkness and light to you are both alike.

Psalm 139:11

What is the dark night of the soul? How does it differ from mental illness, if at all? St. John of the Cross, Spanish mystic and theologian (1542–1591), explained how the "dark night of the soul" is indeed different from depression. In a depression, "a lukewarm person is very lax and remiss in his will and spirit, and has no solicitude about serving God." On the other hand, he indicates that the dark night is different from this: the "person suffering the purgative dryness [dark night] is ordinarily solicitous, concerned and pained about not serving God."[1] In order for the soul to be filled by God, it must be emptied

---

1. John of the Cross, *Dark Night of the Soul* 1.9.3, quoted in Denys Turner, *The Darkness of God* (Cambridge: Cambridge University Press, 1995), 236.

through the dark night and be purged by spiritual experience that, for John of the Cross, was severe in its demands on the self. While his spirituality may seem severe, John was a man of deep charity and faith and wrote beautiful spiritual poetry.

The difference between the dark night and regular depression as diagnosed daily around the world is that even in such a dark night the soul regrets its accidie. It has remorse for its lack of service to God. Should I be happy that at the very least I am pained about not serving God? At least I can claim the dark night of the soul instead of plain vanilla depression. The dark night of the soul can in fact be seen as the mirror image of depression: "Every experience in the one is contained in the other, but everything is reversed."[2]

But is John of the Cross right? Can it really be true that when depression passes, all is restored, but when the dark night passes, all is transformed? How can anyone live through depression, come out the other end, and not be transformed to some extent? I think that patients who are engaged in psychotherapy, if they work hard with the right therapist, cannot help coming out the other end of depression unchanged. But I suppose John of the Cross would respond that the transformation of the soul is what we seek in the Christian life, not merely transformation of the personality. Of course John would know nothing of the assumptions of modern psychotherapy and would not have made such a distinction between personality and soul. But I can, since such concepts are at my disposal. The transformation that happens in the dark night of the soul, of which John had plenty, would be different from the personal transformation that happens in psychotherapy. The dark night of the soul enables one to love God more, while depression (and psychotherapy) can enable one to love the self more in the best of situations. Of course there is no saying that either mental illness or therapy cannot make one love God more, rather simply that the dark night transforms the soul through hardships, which, like John's, can bring great blessings from God. In the end, for what it is worth, I do believe that I have had the soul's dark nights.

Is it possible that God gives us the dark night as a test, to transform us? According to John this is so. We should allow ourselves

2. Ibid., 243.

to be transformed into his likeness. But would God really lead us to conjure up all the methods possible of ending human life? Would God create grotesque, life-denying, dangerous thoughts and visions? Would God so change our joy into mourning that we would want to return the gift of our own life to the Giver, like some unopened Christmas package to a spurned lover? I have a hard time believing all this. I think that these are not of God but of Evil, that power that seeks to do harm to God's creatures, separating them from relation to him. How then could this issue from the dark night?

Of course, to speak of the dark night of the soul is anathema to many in the psychiatric field. I was told by one of my psychiatrists over the years not to equate depression with any religious experience such as the dark night of the soul. I never asked him why; I just assumed that he didn't want religious language to be mixed with medical. I did try to tell him, however, that religious language covers all and every aspect of being, that I could not simply separate it from his profession's language and concepts. He looked disgusted.

Mental illness is a biological disease. It is an event in the brain. Medications and psychotherapy both change the metabolic structure of the brain. Yes, I agree, but so does prayer. And all can be transformed by the dark night.

Julian of Norwich (1342–1416), English mystic of an earlier period than John, says the following of the relation between sorrow and transformation: "Before miracles come sorrow, anguish and tribulation. He does not will that we be overly depressed by the sorrows and storms that come our way, because that has always been the condition before miracles come."

Do any miracles come from mental illness? I suppose that could depend on how we define a miracle. If we understand a miracle as did Augustine (354–430) to be that which causes us to marvel at the power and goodness of God, I can imagine that miracles could indeed result from mental illness. I certainly have known miracles of resurrection to come from my own illness. Not that I would wish mental illness on anyone who was hoping for a miracle—or on anyone who was not. But this does lead me to wonder how we might use Julian's insight as she does, as a way of attempting not to drown in our present sorrow. Psychotropic medication is supposed to relieve the illness itself, as is psychotherapy, which is also supposed to help us understand ourselves, what makes us ill and why. But based on Julian's insight, what should the Christian do in addition to making use of these avenues? Would we need specifically to welcome the sorrow, not seek relief from it? No, I think Julian would say that sorrow in itself is not to be sought out, and relief *is* to be sought, and that from God. Of course, she is the one who said, "All thing shall be well, and all thing shall be well, and all manner of thing shall be well." But the transformation that can come of sorrow is to be welcomed.

> To keep me from being too elated [by an abundance of revelations], a thorn was given me in the flesh, a messenger of Satan to torment me, to keep me from being too elated. Three times I appealed to the Lord about this, that it would leave me, but he said to me, "My grace is sufficient for you, for power is made perfect in weakness."
>
> 2 Corinthians 12:7

I do know that compassion is one of those lessons I must learn from my illness. Doesn't everything boil down to that? God still has much work to do to overcome my being *incurvata in me*, curved in upon myself, the root of sin. I still have far to go there. My struggle with my thorn, my own weakness, is not finished and will never be finished in this life. Who knows what Paul's "thorn" really was? Nobody, really. It may have simply been the trouble he had with the "super-apostles" and the false teachers who were constantly trying to sabotage his ministry for their own pride and power. In any case, there Satan gave the thorn. And there, even there, God did not allow it to be removed but planned to use it for good. Can anything good really ever come of this—a medical disease that can cripple the brain and mind? "Take every thought captive to obey Christ" (2 Corinthians 10:5). Could Paul have known of my condition, which itself is the captor, which itself wrings my mind dry of thoughts of Christ and wants to hand my soul over to hell?

Plenty of Christians before must have had this difficulty, and many Christians probably will after me. Mental illness is not an indication of the weakness of one's faith. It may be, however, a test and should be met like all other tests: with prayer that God will see us through it faithfully, that we will be seen faithful, and that we should be found at the last without reproach, that God will use it to our benefit and us to his glory.

After all, as I have said, faith is not primarily a feeling. It is an activity. Sometimes the most pleasing thing to God is our obedience and rendering of thanks even when we don't feel at all thankful. Jesus said that even the hypocrites love those who love them; they love when it is easy. But the most valuable thing in God's sight is loving the unlovely, loving when one has no love, hoping when hope is not seen. Then we really have to admit that all our loves and all our hopes are ultimately borrowed from God anyway.

> Now the great thing is this: we are consecrated and dedicated to God in order that we may thereafter think, speak, meditate and do, nothing except to his glory. . . . We are not our own: let not our reason nor our will, therefore, sway our plans and deeds. We are not our own: let us therefore not set it as our goal to seek what is expedient for us according to the flesh. We are not our own: in so far as we ,can, let us therefore forget ourselves and all that is ours. Conversely, we are God's: let us therefore live for him and die for him. We are God's: let his wisdom and will therefore rule all our actions. We are God's: let all the parts of our life accordingly strive toward him as our only lawful goal.
>
> John Calvin (1509–1564)
> (cf. Romans 14:7–9; 1 Corinthians 6:19–20)

From a theological perspective, the most dangerous thing about mental illness is that it can lock us in ourselves, convincing us that we are indeed our own, and completely on our own, isolated in our distress. Darkness *is* my only companion. Mental illness is a veil that shrouds our consecration to God, blocking out the glory of the Holy One. Our wounds fester; our remoteness from the source of our healing increases. Mental illness shuts all windows and doors to the soul so that we cannot speak, meditate, or do anything to the glory of God, or so it seems. All is experienced as pain. We are locked in ourselves, unable to forget our pain. How does the Christian endure such remoteness from the source of our life?

> O Lord, calm the waves of this heart; calm its tempests. Calm yourself, O my soul, so that the divine can act in you. Calm yourself,

O my soul, so that God is able to repose in you, so that his peace may cover you. Yes, Father in heaven, often have we found that the world cannot give us peace, O but make us feel that you are able to give peace; let us know the truth of your promise: that the whole world may not be able to take away your peace.

Søren Kierkegaard (1813–1855)

I must value myself, and not disvalue, such as would impoverish my Creator. But if I try to talk this way to my psychiatrist, he may be convinced that I do not value myself at all, that I have to look to the divine "projection" of myself in order to validate myself, give myself reason to be. Here is another place where the chasm between the religious patient and the nonreligious therapist simply cannot be bridged. Is he right? Am I really not valuing myself for myself? Yes, he is right, but the value I put on his being right is the opposite of that which he claims it is. I do not value myself for myself, but this in itself does not necessarily indicate ill-health on my part, spiritually or mentally. I value myself for the One who created and redeemed me and who will raise me on the last day. This is the only true self-affirmation, the only one that makes any sense within biblical and traditional Christianity. Bernard of Clairvaux (1090–1153) says that the highest form of spiritual achievement is learning to love the self for the sake of God.

But one of my psychiatrists can't get it, won't get it, looked at me as if I were some animal from the zoo, as if I had been irredeemably hoodwinked by false consciousness. Without the triune God (as though there were really some "without" where I could stand), I bear only ephemeral value. This is not bad. This is simply true. And by the grace of God, I have been engrafted into Christ's identity in my baptism, and so this truth is not bad news but good news. Incredibly good news. Mental illness veils this news, masks this news. How can a secular psychiatrist help me here? Only in spite of himself, I suppose. Only by the grace of the very God he despises. But I can't give up on the possibility that he could help me. After all, the angel Gabriel said to Mary, "Nothing will be impossible with God" (Luke 1:37), when he announced that she would bear the Christ without having yet "known a man." And as the angel said to Abraham upon hearing Sarah laugh at the promise of a son, "Is anything too hard for

the LORD?" (Genesis 18:14 RSV). Our faith is full of surprises. I
just can't stand the illness that veils them from me.

> He has not dealt with us according to our sins,
>   nor rewarded us according to our wickedness
> For as the heavens are high above the earth,
>   so is his mercy great upon those who fear him.
> As far as the east is from the west,
>   so far has he removed our sins from us.
> As a father cares for his children,
>   so does the LORD care for those who fear him.
> For he himself knows whereof we are made;
>   he remembers that we are but dust.
>
> Psalm 103:10–14

Why is this illness happening? I never ask "Why me?" Only "Why
this?" I respect God's sovereignty to afflict and to comfort whom
he wills, but why this kind of affliction? How can I do your work
in this state? Do the dead praise you?

> My child, do not regard lightly the discipline of the Lord,
>   or lose heart when you are punished by him;
> for the Lord disciplines those whom he loves
>   and chastises every child whom he accepts.
>
> Endure trials for the sake of discipline. God is treating you
>   as children.
>
> Hebrews 12:5–7, quoting Proverbs 3:11–12

Are you disciplining me with madness? Can that really be? I will
try to understand this, because this pain seems so near to the
demonic that I find it hard to understand the discipline of the
Merciful One in it. But I will try to understand. As Hebrews says
earlier, I have not yet resisted the powers of evil to the point of
shedding my blood, to the point of martyrdom for the name of
Jesus. I suppose I should be grateful that my battle is internal
and is not against those who could destroy my body in order to
quench the hope of my soul. But my body does not need to be
destroyed to quench my hope, because inside of me the battle
rages against that very hope, to convince me that that hope is
mere illusion, that pain is all there is. And the interior battle

that strives to quench my hope threatens to destroy my very body. But not in the name of Jesus—against the name of Jesus, in hatred of the name of Jesus. My God, my God, why have you abandoned me?

> Now, discipline always seems painful rather than pleasant at the time, but later it yields the peaceful fruit of righteousness to those who have been trained by it.
>
> Therefore lift your drooping hands and strengthen your weak knees, and make straight paths for your feet, so that what is lame may not be put out of joint, but rather be healed.
>
> Hebrews 12:11–13

Be healed. Lift your drooping hands. Strengthen your weak knees. How can I do that? My hands do nothing but droop. My knees are nothing but weak. "There is no health in my flesh" (Psalm 38:3). How can I be healed? You speak to me in Hebrews as though I could do it myself, as though I had the power to "snap out of this." I seriously doubt this. I have tried, and tried, and will not stop trying even though I want to stop trying. Make straight my paths, you say. I am lame and cannot walk twisted paths. When I sprained my ankle, I literally could not walk except on the most level of surfaces without causing myself pain. What then are straight paths for the sprained brain? Even when you suggest that I see this as discipline (for surely Christians read these ancient texts as speaking directly to us even now), you are not suggesting that I impale myself on the discipline. You tell me to take courage and make sure that I take the straight paths, the way of righteousness that will not hurt my already sprained brain but will help to put the lame places in me right.

> My brothers and sisters, whenever you face trials of any kind, consider it nothing but joy, because you know that the testing of your faith produces endurance; and let endurance have its full effect, so that you may be mature and complete, lacking in nothing.
>
> James 1:2–4

Consider it nothing but joy. My brain disorder itself is supposed to cause me joy? Not because the Christian is meant to flagellate herself, or because we are to look for troubles and tests in life, but trials may be considered cause for joy since they produce endurance and maturity. I wonder what my doctor would think about this.

> My child, do not despise the LORD's discipline
>   or be weary of his reproof,
> for the LORD reproves the one he loves,
>   as a father the son in whom he delights.
>
> Proverbs 3:11–12

Is God really treating me as a child? Surely then it must be like Isaac in Genesis 22, the chosen, the child of the promise, whom God tells Abraham to sacrifice on Mount Moriah. That is the child I am. Not a dear child, not one whom God protects. Yet Isaac was indeed the child of the promise, "Take your son, your only son Isaac, whom you love . . ." (Genesis 22:2) And at the last moment God told Abraham not to slay him. Is this what it means to endure all trials for the sake of discipline? Again, my doctors and therapists would cough, objecting. But still I am told that we are to endure all trials for the sake of discipline. Truly you are a God who hides himself (Isaiah 45:15).

Isaiah's statement that God hides himself is taken up in the history of Christian theology. Martin Luther (1483–1546), the great Reformer, among others, believed that we know God best *sub contrario*, or in his hiddenness. Blaise Pascal (1623–1662), too, worked with this theme of the hiddenness of God in his *Pensées*. For Pascal, "what can be seen on earth points to neither the total absence nor the obvious presence of divinity, but to the presence of a hidden God" (*Pensées* 449). This is because for Pascal, and arguably for Isaiah as well, the existence of God is not obvious to human reason. If God were not hidden in some sense, humanity would not be required to seek assistance in the knowledge of God. This would result in our own hubris and further cut us off from God's presence. In this sense, the hiddenness of God is revelatory.

But when I say that God is a God that hides himself, is this what I mean? Surely hubris and arrogance are not the problem, and human reason is not the problem, and revelation is not the problem. Rather, suffering is the problem. God hides himself from my suffering, in my suffering. My question is this: *How long, O LORD? How long?*

God, give us grace to accept with serenity the things that cannot
be changed, courage to change the things that should be changed,
And the wisdom to distinguish the one from the other.

Reinhold Niebuhr (1892–1971)[3]

I cannot change my health, or lack of it. I have a brain disorder
from which I will never "recover." There is no "cure." There may
be someday; researchers are experimenting with magnets and elec-
tronic implants. But these are not yet available. We have, however,
finally found a constellation of medications that provide me relief
from the deepest and longest depressions, from the randomness of
mania, from the indignity of hearing and seeing things not present.
At this point, I only occasionally have my days when the world is
so bleak that I am dismantled. I usually spend such days either in
agony, still functioning as I must with the children and my respon-
sibilities at church, or by retreating into bed and merciful, forget-
ful sleep. Will I spend my entire life in such blithering antipodes,
between elation and productivity or despair and sleep? At least I
can sleep. Some people have the curse of not even being able to
sleep, having nerves rough hewn from insomnia. *God, give us grace
to accept with serenity the things that cannot be changed . . .*

> I waited patiently upon the LORD,
>   he stooped to me and heard my cry.
> He lifted me out of the desolate pit, out of the mire and clay;
>   he set my feet upon a high cliff and made my footing sure.
> He put a new song in my mouth,
> a song of praise to our God;
>   many shall see, and stand in awe,
>   and put their trust in the LORD. . . .
> Though I am poor and afflicted,
>   the Lord will have regard for me.
> You are my helper and my deliverer;
>   do not tarry, O my God.

Psalm 40:1–3, 18–19

Like Israel brought back from exile, I have been bought with
a price. "You are not your own, you are the Lord's." A fountain

---

3. Elisabeth Sifton, *The Serenity Prayer: Faith and Politics in Times of Peace
and War* (New York: W. W. Norton, 2003), 7.

in an arid land is the Holy Spirit to my soul. If only I could remember when mentally ill that this is true. Maybe this is my vocation in life, praising God even in the midst of humiliation and sheer hatred of self. Or rather, hatred of my condition, but it feels like hatred of self. I plead for compassion for self, for gentleness toward self, but it seems illusory.

> Grant, I beg you, merciful Lord, that the designs of a new and better life, which by your grace I have now formed, may not pass away without effect. Incite and enable me, by your Holy Spirit, to improve the time which you shall grant me; to avoid all evil thoughts, words, and actions; and to do all the duties which you shall set before me. Hear my prayer, O Lord, for the sake of Jesus Christ.
>
> Samuel Johnson (1702–1784)

To improve the time which you shall grant me . . . Gracious and Holy One, give me your mercy to avoid the thoughts in the blackness which separate me from you, which lead only to death. I have no strength of my own to avoid them, to steer around them; my ship is tossed and cast about by the Powers Grim. Please, dear God, have mercy on me, that I may not do that which would permanently separate me from my family, for the sake of my family and to the glory of your name.

> With weeping they shall come,
>   and with consolations I will lead them back,
> I will let them walk by brooks of water,
>   in a straight path in which they shall not stumble;
> for I have become a father to Israel.
>
> Jeremiah 31:9

In such prophecies of redemption I find peace. I find hope. I find comfort. Sometimes all I can do is read scripture, both the Old Testament and the New, and the prayers of the faithful, such as these, just to keep going.

> Blessed be the God and Father of our Lord Jesus Christ, the Father of mercies and the God of all consolation, who consoles us in all our affliction, so that we may be able to console those who are in any affliction with the consolation with which we ourselves are

consoled by God. For just as the sufferings of Christ are abundant for us, so also our consolation is abundant through Christ.

2 Corinthians 1:3–5

This reminds me of God's comfort, of God's tender care, without which I am lost, adrift in my illness. It reminds me of the consolation not only of Christ but also of discipleship. In our discipleship toward others, we learn of the sufferings of Christ and therefore of his care. And this in turn means that we can know and serve the experience of those who also go through adversity and suffering.

These passages give me great comfort. Where is the God of anger, of punishment of sin, the hidden God? Not here.

O Lord, reassure me with your quickening Spirit; without you I can do nothing. Mortify in me all ambition, vanity, vainglory, worldliness, pride, selfishness and resistance to God, and fill me with love, peace, and all the fruits of the Spirit. O Lord, I know not what I am, but to you I flee for refuge. I would surrender myself to you, trusting your precious promises and against hope believing in hope. You are the same yesterday, today, and for ever; and therefore, waiting on the Lord, I trust I shall at length renew my strength.

William Wilberforce (1759–1833)

Mortify in me all ambition. I cannot work as I would. I am unreliable, my worst fear and disillusionment. I have had to back out of speaking engagements again this year. This decision was exquisitely difficult for me. Hard because of my self-image, and exquisite because as I made the decisions to back out, I breathed a prayer of mercy and thanks. My self-image is of a strong woman, capable of taking on and taking on and taking on. I can no longer be thus. I must now be more realistic, relying on the power of the Holy Spirit to "mortify in me all vanity, vainglory, worldliness, pride, selfishness and resistance to God . . ." To fall into God's hands is a wondrous thing.

> I lift up my eyes to the hills;
>   from where is my help to come?
> My help comes from the LORD,
>   the maker of heaven and earth.

He will not let your foot be moved,
and he who watches over you will not fall asleep.
Behold, he who keeps watch over Israel
shall neither slumber nor sleep;
The LORD himself watches over you;
the LORD is your shade at your right hand,
So that the sun shall not strike you by day,
nor the moon by night.
The LORD shall preserve you from all evil;
it is he who shall keep you safe.
The LORD shall watch over your going out and your coming in,
from this time forth for evermore.

Psalm 121

I once asked a rabbi I knew if he believed this, that the One who watches over Israel shall neither slumber nor sleep. I am sure that some rabbis do believe this, but this one answered that he did not and could not believe it. If God watched over Israel, how could the Holocaust have happened? Now—not to trivialize that horrendous event of history—I have had my own burnt offering to the Lord, and how can I believe that God does not sleep through my pain? Does the Lord really watch our going out and coming in? I have to answer yes. I must answer positively because scripture witnesses that indeed God does not sleep, does watch, does preserve us. The question then is how? why? when? But not *if* . . .

You who fear the Lord, wait for his mercy;
and turn not aside, lest you fall.
You who fear the Lord, trust in him,
and your reward will not fail;
You who fear the Lord, hope for good things,
for everlasting joy and mercy.

Sirach 2:7–9

Hope. When we are in a state of severe mental illness, hope is far from us. This is why we need the scriptures and the community of faith. They contribute faith and hope to us as from a well we cannot now reach. We do see that the well is there. We must grab on to the hope of the community, to the faith and trust of the people of God, which is objectively there whether we can feel it or not.

> Take off the garment of your sorrow and affliction, O Jerusalem, and put on for ever the beauty of the glory from God. Put on the robe of righteousness from God; put on your head the diadem of the glory of the Everlasting.
>
> Baruch 5:1–2

Slowly I am taking off the garment of my sorrow and affliction, because of medication, a caring therapist, an excellent psychiatrist, a loving and patient husband, two children, friends and family who love me, and lots of prayer. Despite my frequent desires, I will not leave my family by harming myself irreparably. Taking off the garment of sorrow and affliction here appears to be something that Jerusalem is doing herself, something she is commanded to do on her own. I must do this actively, on my own. I must fight the depressions with every ounce of courage and strength. *Put on for ever the beauty of the glory from God.*

> Why do you say, O Jacob,
>   and speak, O Israel,
> "My way is hid from the LORD,
>   and my right is disregarded by my God"?
> Have you not known? Have you not heard?
> The LORD is the everlasting God,
>   the Creator of the ends of the earth.
> He does not faint or grow weary;
>   his understanding is unsearchable.
> He gives power to the faint
>   and strengthens the powerless.
> Even youths will faint and be weary,
>   and the young will fall exhausted;
> but they who wait upon the LORD shall renew their strength,
>   they shall mount up with wings like eagles,
> they shall run and not be weary,
>   they shall walk and not faint.
>
> Isaiah 40:27–31

Strength is not even necessarily to the young, nor health to the youthful, but those who serve the LORD will glorify the LORD in

waiting upon him. Teach me, LORD, to wait. My health is in waiting upon you, serving you, praising you all my days.

> Because God did not make death,
> he does not delight in the death of the living.
>
> Wisdom of Solomon 1:13

I cannot believe that God wills death or sickness. In the Garden
of Eden, the first pair was warned that "in the day that you eat
of [the fruit of the tree of the knowledge of Good and of Evil]
you shall die" (Genesis 2:17). This is not God's will. God sets his
commandment over them, and they break it. Only with their
reaching out and eating of the tree do they become subject to
evil and death, of course with God's forewarning.

So I cannot believe that God wills my necrotizing brain to
kill me, even when I am convinced that death would be the least
painful exit. *God does not delight in the death of the living.* "God
intended it for good . . ." (Genesis 50:20).

> You will forget your misery;
> you will remember it as waters that have passed away.
> And your life will be brighter than the noonday;
> its darkness will be like the morning.
> And you will have confidence, because there is hope;
> you will be protected and take your rest in safety.
> You will lie down, and no one will make you afraid;
> many will entreat your favor.
>
> Job 11:16–19

Just as it was the memories of Israel and the church that buoyed
me during my illness, so now I need to forget: to forget my misery, to remember it as waters that have passed away. My life will
indeed be brighter than the noonday; I will be protected and
take my rest in safety. Just as before I needed to remember the
mercies of God in the past, now I must forget the suffering and
evil of my illness, in order to let God heal and protect me.

> Even though you, my enemies, intended to do me harm, God
> intended it for good . . .
>
> Genesis 50:20

Can I really say that God intended it for good—this pain, this wretchedness, this humiliation? If all of God's intentions for us are good, why do we suffer? Luther said we suffer because of the grace of God. I have a hard time believing this. I think we suffer because of evil, the deprivation of the good, but even still God can work out of suffering his grace.

> Batter my heart, three person'd God; for you
> As yet but knock, breathe, shine, and seek to mend;
> That I may rise, and stand, o'erthrow me, and bend
> Your force to break, blow, burn, and make me new.
>
> John Donne (1572–1631)

Take up your battering ram, loving Lord, and splinter the gates of my heart. Do not knock gently. Behold, I stand at the door and I wait for your knocking. Please, dear God, there is nothing I desire more, for nothing else will lead to my health but your force. Make me new. Make me new. Renew me.

II

Health and Prayer

I waited patiently upon the Lord;
  he stooped to me and heard my cry.
He lifted me out of the desolate pit, out of the mire and clay;
  he set my feet upon a high cliff and made my footing sure.

Psalm 40:1–2

Be not afraid to pray—
to pray is right.
Pray, if thou canst, with hope;
But ever pray,
Though hope be weak
or sick with long delay;
Pray in the darkness,
if there be no light.

Hartley Coleridge, 1796–1849

Pray? Pray? Are you kidding? My mind is mush, jello, the leavings at the bottom of the garbage can. How can I pray? I don't even want to. I am steamed, furious, sputtering angry. Pray with hope, my foot. Pray in the darkness? Well, that would be the only place I could pray, because there is no light, but even there I can't pray, not now and apparently never again. I will never get better. I am simply going progressively mad. Tick by tock by tick, with each turn of the clock's gears I am closer to insanity. And you tell me to pray. I am just glad you prayed, Hartley Coleridge, you, Hebrews, you, King David, because I can't. I will pray your prayers, lean on your faith. I have none of my own.

> Ah, Lord, my prayers are dead, my affections dead, and my heart is dead.
> But thou art a living God and I bear myself upon thee.
>
> William Bridge (1600–1670)

I was cleaning up the garden to try to keep myself busy, to try to keep the pain of the latest depression at bay. Busyness is an important part of healing, or at least staving off, the symptoms of depressive disorder. I had been piling the daylily leaves, long, golden-brown, and spent, on the grass by the garage as I pulled more. I went to the pile to throw away another armful and noticed that the scrolling leaves spelled "Jesus." I blinked, glanced back, and the letters spelling out my Lord's name were gone, receded into the pile of so many leaves.

I am supposed to be getting better. Why is this still happening? Then I realized that the word I saw was not like the severed fingers of my daughter, nor like the highway rolling up in smoke. This was a good vision, a nonthreatening vision. I asked myself why I would be seeing that word, *Jesus*, and not another. Then an old hymn came to my mind.

> What a friend we have in Jesus,
> All our sins and griefs to bear,
> We must never be discouraged,
> Take it to the Lord in prayer.
> Do thy friends despise, forsake thee?
> Is there trouble ev'rywhere?
> Jesus knows our every weakness,
> Thou wilt find a solace there.
>
> Joseph M. Scriven (1820–1886)

And it cheered me. Consoled me. *Thou wilt find a solace there.* Jesus can heal the soul even while using the sickness of the brain.

Darkness is not my only companion. *What a friend we have in Jesus.* The kind who won't leave us. Why did it take me so long to remember this?

I had not been praying for my own healing at this point. I do not mean to generalize and say that all mentally ill people should follow me in this. But the only prayer I could muster was for strength to endure this. There were of course times when the shadow of an inkling crossed my mind to pray for healing, but for some reason it did not seem the right thing to do. How strange. It just didn't fit. Almost as if it were blasphemous to pray for healing, to be rid of despair, to be freed of the horror of bouncing from high to low. I am not called to pray for healing from this, only for strength to endure. This is because I believe that God still has much to teach me through this, and that some of what he will teach I can't even yet begin to imagine.

> For surely I know the plans I have for you, says the LORD, plans for your welfare and not for harm, to give you a future with hope. Then when you call upon me and come and pray to me, I will hear you. When you search for me, you will find me; if you seek me with all your heart, I will let you find me, says the LORD, and I will restore your fortunes and gather you from all the nations and all the places where I have driven you, says the LORD, and I will bring you back to the place from which I sent you into exile.
>
> Jeremiah 29:11–14

But now I can pray. God has let me find him. Health begins to shine through the pain. It feels like water on parched lips, like salve on a wound. I cannot believe how sick I was, how beginning to be "normal" feels so amazing.

What was the worth of being sick? While before I felt like a mouse being batted about by a huge cat, now I feel healing. And I feel that God is the ultimate source of that healing, even though medications and therapy are part of it. What was God's relation to my suffering? In what sense did he cause or allow my suffering, and to what end? This is a central question for the Christian who suffers from mental illness: What is God's relationship to my pain?

It seems to me that the answer is that God is present throughout, even when it doesn't feel like it. It also can feel as if God is the author of the pain, because so much learning goes on throughout and in the suffering. But how can I say that God causes suffering? Maybe, as with Job, God allows the suffering as a test. I have indeed been tested as by fire. What, then, is the relationship between the sufferings of Christ and the Christian sufferer? "I am now rejoicing in my sufferings for your sake, and in my flesh I am completing what is lacking in Christ's affliction for the sake of his body, that is, the church" (Colossians 1:24). For the writer of Colossians, there is clearly a relationship between his own sufferings and Christ's sufferings, in such a positive relationship that they work to the well-being of the body of Christ. This is cause for rejoicing. After all, how can one complete what is lacking in Christ's affliction except with rejoicing? I do not easily rejoice in my sufferings per se, but here if I follow the apostle I must rejoice, insofar as they are mini-reflections of the redeeming suffering of Christ. They redound to the benefit of the body. And I do hope that this is true. But if I were to keep quiet about my sufferings, this would not be true. It might be a benefit to me, but not to those around me.

Those who are healthy, who have never been sick, will not know the joy and release and comfort God gives us in health. You have to be sick in order to know the joy of health. You have to be, or at least feel, cut off from the body in order to benefit from its community. Not necessarily mentally ill, of course, but truly ill, sick unto death.

> Comfort, O comfort my people,
>   says your God.
> Speak tenderly to Jerusalem,
>   and cry to her
> that she has served her term,
>   that her penalty is paid,
> that she has received from the Lord's hand
>   double for all her sins.
>
> Isaiah 40:1–2

Comfort here was for the people as a whole, for a nation whose warfare will be over and whose sin forgiven. To read it as addressed to me, in the singular, is not to make a category error; truly scripture speaks in more ways than a straightforward way, even while our understanding is based on a plain reading. There is nothing that violates the scripture here for me to take this comfort on myself, to claim it as my own, now in the twenty-first century. I read this passage as comfort to me, not only to Israel, not only to the present Israel of God, the church of Jews and Gentiles.

How do I understand my sufferings in relation to God, except through prayer? Prayer has been for me a large comfort, both my own prayers and the prayers of others on my behalf. However, those prayers on my behalf were fewer than they could have been, since I did not tell many people what was wrong. This is part of the tragedy of the stigma of mental illness for the Christian. There was one friend, though, who prayed for me faithfully and constantly for years, to whom I will always be grateful. And of course, my family and a few other friends who also knew of my illness supported me in prayer.

There have been studies of the efficacy of prayer that have led even the scientific world to admit that there could be something important there for the healing of body, mind, and soul. For example, Harvard researchers surveyed more than two thousand adults, finding that prayer helped in more cases than did visits to the doctor for depression, anxiety disorders, arthritis, back pain, and cancer. A well-known experiment by cardiologist Randolph Boyd likewise showed the importance of prayer in healing. In this double-blind, randomized experiment, some patients were prayed for and some were not. Patients, nurses, and doctors did not know which patients were in which group. The results showed that the prayed-for patients had a markedly lesser need for antibiotics, they were less likely to develop pulmonary edema, and none of them needed intubation.[1] Of course, the Christian faith does not depend on such studies to value prayer.

I have always been very wary of "faith healers." Liberal Christianity has been an influence on me since my youth in this regard, and it tends to shy away from the idea that prayer

1. Larry Dossey, *Healing Words: The Power of Prayer and the Practice of Medicine* (New York: HarperPaperbacks, 1993), 248–49.

would be truly effective. Faith healers remind me of hucksters. Not all healers are alike, however, and not all are hucksters. We invited one who worked in the Diocese of Connecticut to our parish for a healing workshop. He stressed that the prayers would begin the healing process but that healing would rarely be a dramatic event. The workshop involved at one point gathering the congregation around one person at a time and praying with the laying on of hands. When it was my turn, I sat in the chair at the center of the crowd, and they put their hands on me, and those who couldn't reach me laid their hands on those in front of them. They began to pray. I do not remember the specific words Nigel used, but I was overwhelmed. In part it was that all those people were around me, praying for me, and I felt a deep gratitude and tenderness. In part it was that I felt all those years of blackness being pulled out of me. I wept. I don't know how long this lasted. Maybe ten minutes or longer. All I know is that since then I have been doing better and better all the time, despite my previous judgments of this type of healing.

Now, I would never use this experience as an excuse to stop seeing my therapist or to cut off the medication. Even though there have certainly been times that I have wanted to do this, this desire has come from a perverse need for independence from my medications and therapists rather than the feeling that I had been healed by prayer.

In addition, I would never want to suggest by relating this experience that prayer is a tool to be used at one's whim for the betterment of life. Of course it is indeed for the betterment of life, and of course it is one of the "spiritual tools" that the Christian relies upon, but it is never to be understood in an instrumental sense. That is, in prayer we are not to "heap up empty phrases" like the hypocrites in order to twist God's arm into action (Matt. 6:7). This is blasphemy. But for the Christian, prayer is our relationship with God, and it is proper that we make our requests known to God. It is appropriate to hope and ask for healing, but it is not theologically correct to assume that we can manipulate the power of God in our prayers.

Since prayer is key to the Christian's relationship with God, it will naturally bring health in God's good time. To be brought into relationship with the living God, to be able to touch the fringe of Jesus's prayer shawl, works in us God's curative power. It may be on the other side of illness, through the path of the dark night and past difficult experiences. But to know God is eternal life. Prayer will bring health—even for the bent and broken mind of the mentally ill.

Part Three

Living with Mental Illness

12

How Clergy, Friends, and Family Can Help

He will feed his flock like a shepherd;
  he will gather the lambs in his arms,
and carry them in his bosom,
  and gently lead the mother sheep.

Isaiah 40:11

I was visited by two clergy members, both friends, during one of my stays in the hospital. They came and stayed, and stayed. I think they thought I must be bored and needed entertaining. Fact was, I was so tired. I just gave my tight, skin-stretching smile and nodded while they chatted away.

I think people in general don't know how to treat the mentally ill. They are too nervous and uncomfortable to understand that the mental hospital is a respite for the mentally ill and that visitation should be kept to a maximum of ten to fifteen minutes. This probably goes for the physically ill as well. While people may think that the hospital is a boring place and that the patient needs conversation, in fact hospitals can be exhausting. Nurses and roommates, not to mention side effects of new medications, are constantly interrupting sleep. For the mental patient, talking to anyone can be testing.

The visitor should always inquire after the health of the patient. Don't start complaining about your own problems or even someone else's just to have something to talk about. Follow the patient's lead. If she wants to talk about meaningful things such as her symptoms, fears, and worries, then inquire further. But don't pry. Remember that for the mental patient conversation, especially when hospitalized, can be an uphill battle.

Offer to read scripture. Invite the patient to indicate her own requests, but do not press here either, as making decisions is often difficult for the mental patient. Psalm 139 was and remains a comfort to me. Offer to pray. If you have an oil stock, offer unction. If you have a Communion kit, offer Communion. But that should be about all. Be out of there fifteen minutes later to leave the patient to recover, unless she requests a longer visit. Come about once a week while the patient is hospitalized, unless she requests otherwise. That is, don't leave her alone in the hospital.

How can clergy help a mentally ill parishioner before hospitalization has become necessary? This is tricky, because clergy may not be aware either of the symptoms to watch for or of the parishioner's own constellation of problems. The most obvious thing to watch for is tears. Do you notice that anyone in particular is consistently tearing up during the hymns, say, or prayers? Are you aware of any familial problems or causes for grief? If not, or maybe even if so, it may be depression peeking out. Not necessarily, but maybe. Have you noticed that this person is less communicative, smiles less frequently, is either gaining or losing weight noticeably? You may have identified someone in a depression. The question is now: what to do?

What I personally have done is simply to drop the person an e-mail, which is less personal and possibly therefore less threatening than a phone call or a face-to-face communication. This may mean that the parishioner will feel more at ease to divulge her feelings. But if not, then I invite the person out for coffee or lunch. It is, after all, an important part of pastoral care to inquire about the state of a parishioner's soul and mind, in part to keep in touch, in part to know what to pray for. During face-to-face communication, however, do not push and prod. Allow the person time to talk. Be warm and understanding but not too chatty. If you suspect depression, ask the parishioner openly about this. She may have already sought out the help of a therapist. In case not, have in your address book a list of references of therapists whom you trust and have checked out in advance. Keep in touch with the parishioner about this, pray for her, and let her know you are praying for her.

Signs to look for when dealing with mania are odd behaviors, such as changed forms of speech, either pressured or excessive. Look for changes in dressing, such as excessively flamboyant clothing on someone who normally does not wear such. Look for overflowing ideas, evidence of excessive spending, or hyper-sexuality. Look for aggressiveness, enormous energy level, and paranoia. Mania may be easier to spot than depression, since its symptoms are so outward and depression's are more inward.

What should you look for when concerned about schizoaffective disorder? This parishioner will have surreal experiences, divorced from reality. There may be psychotic symptoms such as visions or hallucinations or auditory experiences. What is the difference between a vision and a hallucination? This again is difficult. A psychiatrist would say they are the same but would most probably use the language of hallucination. I would say that a vision can have theological content and can convey a message from God to the person. Hallucinations, though, are often frightening and may have little spiritual or psychological meaning attached to them. They are often nonsense—literally, lacking sense. In the history of Christian spirituality there have been many who have had visions in the above sense, distinguished from hallucinations. The psychiatrist, however, will not usually acknowledge the difference, and religious visions are usually understood as suspect when diagnosing mental illness. In any case, schizophrenia is impossible to diagnose from the pastor's armchair, and psychiatric help should be sought immediately. Some of the symptoms of schizoaffective disorder can occur in severe depression and mania, such as hallucinations, visions, and auditory experiences, and this makes it doubly hard to identify the source.

What if you are dealing with a case of potential suicide or danger to others? This is trickier still. Hopefully the parishioner will open up to you. Signs to watch for are morbid talk of death, either their own or another's, giving away prized possessions, burn or razor tracks on the arms or Band-Aids covering up potential wounds, and, especially, admitting to wanting to hurt hurself or someone else. Take with utmost seriousness any such talk. You now must recommend that the parishioner immediately seek psychiatric help, and you may even contact a close relative, if this was not divulged under the seal of confession, or directly help the parishioner to get this assistance. If there are no family or friends available and no doctor or therapist, you are now responsible for the person's safety.

If this should go far enough, you may have to be involved in an intervention on behalf of your parishioner. This could mean, with her consent and that of her family if nearby, driving her to the hospital and helping her check in. This is the best-case scenario. If things get truly beyond your capacity, there is no immediate psychiatric help, and the parishioner is resistant, you may have to call 911 to have the person committed. This will put a terrible strain on your relationship with that parishioner; I know, because I have unfortunately had to be involved in such an intervention. However, your parishioner's safety is more important than your relationship with her at this point. Do not feel guilty for intervening this way if you must. How would you feel if, God forbid, your parishioner were to kill herself or someone else and you had done nothing to prevent it?

By calling 911, you will set off a chain of reactions that neither you nor your parishioner will be able to undo or stop, so make absolutely certain that you know what you are doing. You cannot send the ambulance away once it has come. In some states, the police and the ambulance will both come to the scene. This will be frightening both for you (*Did I do the right thing?*) and for your parishioner (*Why are the police coming after me?*). At this point your parishioner becomes a patient, and the responsibility is no longer in your hands. If the patient is in a manic or schizophrenic state, be prepared for handcuffs or straitjacket and possibly a scuffle. The police are there in case the patient is uncontrollable, and they will then remove her to the ambulance.

You may choose to go with the ambulance. This may help calm the patient. Once at the hospital, do not be alarmed by the people you may see in the psychiatric emergency room. They may be threatening to you, but remember that they are potentially someone else's parishioners and are someone else's children. It is best to look at the mentally ill this way.

The pastor is thus an important figure here, because he may be the first to know of a parishioner's illness. The clergyperson, however, does not share the skills and knowledge of a psychiatrist and never should try to engage in psychotherapy with someone who is truly mentally ill unless he has the proper qualifications (for example, as a licensed clinical social worker). This may appear objectionable to those pastoral counselors who feel competent, but those with severe mental illness should see a psychiatrist who can administer medication and keep an eye on the patient's progress. This is true even if the patient sees someone else, a social worker or a psychologist, for therapy. One way the clergy can support the parishioner, however, would be to meet regularly in pastoral care or spiritual direction, since the process of therapy itself can be confusing and difficult. Since therapy is usually done from the standpoint of a secular therapist, religious issues may come up that the therapist may not be trained to handle. If the parishioner invites you to engage in this way, consider yourself part of the therapeutic team, but never attempt to handle such a case all by yourself. You must not attempt to fill the role of psychiatrist or therapist. You have your own role.

As for friends, the most useful thing a friend can do is keep in constant contact with the mentally ill patient. This is true whether or not the person is suicidal. To know that your friend remains your friend even though you are mentally ill, or even before you know that, when you think you are just miserable and grumpy, is a great aid toward health. A phone call, a lunch, or even an e-mail can bolster a sagging mood. Don't expect your mentally ill friend, however, to be fun to be with. It is important for you to realize that the friend's poor mental health may look like rejection of friendship, but it is not really this. It is just a sick brain, barely functioning.

Children should be allowed to have a role in their parent's comforting. Most children tend to think that a parent's illness or injury is their own fault. This is dangerous in turn for the child's mental health. While the parent who is mentally ill must not blame herself for her child's difficulties, it is important to think of the children and give them age-appropriate roles in caring for the parent. My own children, once we realized it was best to be open with them, had their own role in helping Mommy. This gave them a sense of power in an otherwise overwhelming situation. My daughter at age three read fluently. She would read to me on the couch, on the bed, anywhere it was quiet and warm. This was somewhat of an annoyance, to tell the truth, because I just wanted to be alone, but I knew it was important for her to play an active role in making Mommy feel better. With my son it was harder, since he was generally angry with me for feeling bad, but we would play quietly with Legos. This too was not the easiest for me, but I knew he enjoyed doing this with me and it made our relationship more normal. Having said this, I must add that children should be reminded that they are not "the Mommy" and do not have the responsibility of mothering her.

Another fact to mention is that you may need to consider putting the children in therapy. I know this sounds over the top if you are not used to the idea of therapy at all. But having a parent ill is like having one flat wheel in the family car, which throws out of kilter the whole. Some families may choose family therapy or couples therapy in addition to the children's therapy. We found all of these extremely important at different times throughout my illnesses.

When the situation is an ill pastor or priest, it can be very difficult for the congregation to confront him or her. People may recognize unusual behavior but may take it personally instead of helping the clergyperson. Sometimes pastors and priests have difficulty allowing themselves to be pastored. I think they often rely on the power of helping others to feel good about themselves. This is dangerous: if a power trip is what one needs, being a pastor or priest will not, and should not, and indeed cannot, be the solution. I wonder, though, how many pastors, priests, and ministers we would actually be left with if those who had such a tendency were to give up their vocation. Certainly it is true that no one can pastor others without admitting his or her own weaknesses. But when pastors seek help from their parishioners, the result is most often disastrous. Unfortunately, denominations that have no place for the office of the bishop sometimes have few ready means for pastoring pastors. If there is a bishop, contact the bishop. If not, contact the appropriate judicatory.

Being a friend or clergy to a mentally ill individual can be difficult. Because of the stigma of mental illness, the ill person may not feel able to open up to you. Do not be offended. Be consistent in your concern, prayer, and inquiries. Let them know that your friendship, or care as a clergyperson, is unconditional. And remember, since mental illness can be a terminal disease, you may be helping to improve or even to save a life.

13

Choosing Therapy

Protect me, O God, for I take refuge in you;
I have said to the LORD, "You are my Lord,
my good above all other."

Psalm 16:1

There is a segment of Christianity in America that still is afraid of therapy, especially conducted by secular therapists.[1] Christians may tend to turn away from psychotherapy because they do not trust secular therapists. The secular therapist often approaches religion from a worldview that is foreign to the Christian. This secular worldview in the West tends to be informed by, in addition to others, Sigmund Freud (1856–1939), Karl Marx (1818–1883), and Ludwig Feuerbach

1. "Christians who turn from God and His word to psychotherapies for help with depression forsake 'the fountain of living waters' to drink from the polluted and unsatisfying and even harmful 'broken cisterns, that can hold no water' (Jeremiah 13)" (Dave Hunt, *Beyond Seduction* [Eugene, OR: Harvest House, 1987], quoted in Timothy R. Phillips and Mark R. McMinn, introduction to *Care for the Soul: Exploring the Intersection of Psychology and Theology* (Downers Grove, IL: InterVarsity Press, 2001), 12.

(1804–1872). Freud believed that religion is a crutch to help us deal with the ultimate reality of our death. Marx stated that religion is the opiate of the masses, used by those in power to control those without power. Feuerbach understood God to be simply "man writ large" and projected onto a cosmic screen, somewhat like the Wizard of Oz in the scene where his identity is revealed by Toto. Certainly Freud, Marx, and Feuerbach are not the only voices informing modern secular psychotherapies; their views even underlie some of liberal Christianity's assessments of religion.

It is therefore sometimes claimed that the only appropriate therapist for a Christian is another Christian. The argument goes as follows: since a non-Christian therapist will have a foreign worldview, there will be no bridge in communication between the therapist and patient. I do not necessarily agree; I do feel that it is highly important for the Christian to have a therapist who is not antagonistic to the Christian faith, but this is not impossible to find among secular therapists. It may be a challenge, but it is certainly possible if the secular therapist is open enough to the Christian's worldview.

Indeed, Christians sometimes reject therapy *in toto*, claiming that all they need for health, and mental health specifically, is Jesus, and then things will be fine. I had a student once who interpreted her own depression as a preconversion illness that disappeared upon her conversion. Maybe so, but what about those of us who have a vibrant faith and a strong relationship with Jesus and yet are still thrown into the pit? Surely the voice of the psalmist throughout reflects the plight of these mentally ill, as it does the plight of the physically ill, the poor, the outcast.

A friend told me recently that it is a betrayal of one's confession of Christ to seek psychiatric help or therapy of any kind. This seems to be a not uncommon perception, especially among evangelical and orthodox Christians. Why is this so? Do we not believe that Satan can work through the biochemistry of our brain or through our family relationships, our childhood, our self-image, to undo us? Satan takes advantage of whatever lies around to set us off. So why shouldn't God be able to use a psychiatrist, even an atheist psychiatrist, to help in the healing process? Maybe the assumption is that God is not capable of this. I don't see why God's grace cannot come in the form of a daily dosage of antidepressant or in the form of a therapist, even an atheist. That cannot be impossible, surely.

You know the old joke. The drowning man sees a surfer going by, who leans out with a hand extended. "Hang on, I'll get you to safety!"

"No," replies the floundering man, "God will save me!"

Next comes a sailboat, and a ring attached to a line is tossed out. "Hang on, we'll get you to safety!"

"No," replies the floundering man, "God will save me!"

Finally, a helicopter appears hovering overhead and a line is let down. "Hang on, we'll get you to safety!" shouts a voice from above.

"No," replies the floundering man, "God will save me!"

Thereupon, the man drowns. At the pearly gates, he meets St. Peter and asks accusingly why God did not save him from drowning. Peter replies, "Look, we sent you a surfer, a sailboat, and a helicopter. What more did you want?"

Maybe at the heart of the objection to therapy is that we are ashamed to admit that we can't handle illness, especially mental illness, on our own. It can be a devastating blow to one's sense of self, after all, to admit to mental unrest. But when we have a bad cough we are usually not similarly ashamed. Why, when we are mentally ill, should we not react with the same dispatch in calling the doctor as we would when we find a lump in the breast?

The answer is, of course, because of the stigma involved. But what makes us think the Christian can or should be able to handle such difficulties alone, much less any other difficulty? The assumption that one can go it alone is at heart Pelagianism. This was the position of a certain theologian, Pelagius, in the fourth century, whom St. Augustine corrected by saying that grace is solely God's doing and we cannot even take the first steps toward God's saving will on our own. Pelagianism shrank the grace of God.

I once heard a psychiatrist disaffected from his own field say that "God is the best psychotherapist." I steamed at hearing that. God is no psychotherapist, except only very broadly, in the etymological sense that God heals (*therapeuo*) our souls (*psyche*). But God heals souls only because God is the One who creates the soul in the first place. God is in this respect quite unlike any therapist I know! Expecting God to be like a psychotherapist is in fact sacrilege, blasphemy. God is not a tool to be used to meet our needs. God does, however, give us tools. Maybe when we are depressed or manic or schizoaffective God has in mind for our use a tool such as a psychotherapist and/or a psychiatrist.

How many therapists and psychiatrists have treated me? The first was a warm and patient intern, a student of psychiatry who arranged for me to be seen for the whole academic year instead of having the requisite cutoff at six weeks. Dr. E. was not a practicing Christian that I could tell, but she tried to be sympathetic to my religious language. Yet I remember her asking me in a dubious manner whether or not I believed that the tongues of fire on the apostles at Pentecost were "real." What did "real" mean? My response made her doubt my sanity more, I think. Even so, I think she understood at least that my religious life was all of me, not just a part. I missed her terribly when I graduated from Yale and was removed from the health plan.

Then I saw Dr. S., whose office was full of plants but whose heart was hardened to anything religious, including me. At least it appeared that he disdained me. Never see a therapist if you sense such a response. The therapeutic relationship cannot be nurtured, even when the fact of the feeling is brought up for discussion. "Why is it important that I should be sympathetic with your religious life?" Such psychobabble. *Only because it is my entire world, you creep.* Here is an example of a secular therapist who can be damaging to the Christian. I hate to say this, because I wanted to believe that anybody of any background should be able to engage in therapy with the Christian. I no longer think that. Therapists who are dogmatically Feuerbachian, who believe that God is "man writ large," will simply not be able to get far with the Christian who disagrees unless they are very disciplined in keeping their own worldview restrained. If they cannot do this, they may do the Christian patient much psychological and spiritual damage.

Then I moved on to an LCSW (licensed clinical social worker), a caring and empathic woman who has fought hard with me and for me over the last nine years, even and especially when I just wanted her to give up. B. has been my adviser and my enemy, my blessing and my bane. There were times I just wanted her to give up on me, but of course she would not. I have loved her deeply for her gentle yet firm care.

As I found out only after beginning therapy with her, she is a Christian of my own denomination, although I do not know the extent of her personal religious life. She has a graduate theological education from the same institution from which I received mine, so we have a common vocabulary. I feel for the most part free to talk about any religious matters, even though she clearly does not agree with me on all topics. Who would? But our therapy is not "Christian" in orientation. She does not pray with me, although she does pray for all of her patients outside the context of the therapeutic session. ("How could I take care of all of you all alone?") She does not encourage or discourage any particular set of religious or spiritual practices for the healing of mental illness. While she is not a "Christian therapist," she is a therapist who is a Christian and a person of prayer, and I feel that God has clearly drawn me into her orbit for healing. She is my angel of mercy.

While seeing her, after I left Dr. S., I had been receiving medication for depression, Zoloft, from my general practitioner, Dr. M. Then I slipped into mania, and B. insisted that I see a psychiatrist for medication. Apparently the Zoloft had tipped me from depression to mania. This is why I believe that psychiatrists are best for prescribing medication, not general practitioners, even if you do not use the psychiatrist for therapy. Psychiatrists are much more aware of the side effects of medications and know what to look for in their patients' demeanor and affect. I wonder whether, if I had been medicated by a psychiatrist instead of a general practitioner, I would have flipped into mania. Maybe a psychiatrist would have been able to identify the signs in advance of the mania. B. was very wise to get me in to see the psychiatrist immediately.

"Nobody doesn't like Dr. K." Well, I must have been the first of the nobodies. He was all right at first, very kind and caring, with a good sense of humor. He even would go overtime if I was particularly distressed, something that most psychiatrists wedded to their fifty-minute hour will not do. While he seemed at first to accept, even if he too could not understand, the religious stuff, he did one day make a comment that I had better not try to interpret my illness through religious language. He said it with a little snort.

While Dr. K. was compassionate for the most part, I began to feel less confident about his care. His office looked like the

Titanic in a tornado: file stacks sliding all over the floor, papers spilling out. Who is not being helped here? What—or who—is falling through the cracks? I soon found that person was myself. When Dr. Disorganization did not return my phone calls during two medical crises, I finally found another psychiatrist. It is very wrenching to take leave of a psychiatrist or therapist, even when you know you have to. So I had to wait until I was feeling better, and I suppose Dr. K. just thought that I was already over his neglect of my care. Instead, I just had to feel strong enough to say goodbye.

Now I see the psychiatrist who administered my ECT in the hospital. I see him for a fifteen-minute session every six weeks for medication, and, unlike with Dr. K., the insurance covers the sessions except for a small copay. Dr. O. looks like Einstein. White hair everywhere. He owns a zany bike with a chair for a seat and the front wheel extended far forward of the frame. He rides it all over town, to the hospital, to the office. He, too, is caring and compassionate, if self-avowedly eccentric, and also has a good sense of humor, an important characteristic for me. He is also internationally renowned for his skills. Dr. O. has brought up religion on occasion, joking for instance about the trouble that the Episcopal Church has had since voting at General Convention in 2003 to consecrate a "practicing" openly gay bishop. I immediately shut off discussion, telling him he wouldn't understand. "But psychiatrists are supposed to understand!" Oh, well.

Then there were all the doctors and social workers and nurses in the hospitals who treated me. For the most part they followed a strictly medical model, not even engaging in therapy. In Yale Psychiatric Institute (YPI) there was little therapy at all. So their attitude toward the religious life did not come out much. But they were amused that I was trying so hard to say Morning and Evening Prayer. I think they were even a bit concerned.

Another social worker whom I saw with the whole family was an excellent therapist. He saw the family in different constellations: the children, Matthew and me, all four of us, Matthew alone, but never me alone. He respected my therapeutic relationship with B. and didn't want to confuse things there. As far as I could tell he was not a practicing Christian, but he tried hard to understand my religious framework. C. was very insightful, practical, and didn't waste any time with us. He is an instance of a social worker whom I would recommend to any parishioner, even though I do not know his own personal belief system. He is able to keep it appropriately under wraps.

I now am engaged in a therapy group in addition to seeing B. The facilitator of the group is a religious Jew. S. is quite open to questions of religious life and the relationship between that and mental health. She sees this to be a positive relation, believing that religious life does not fight against but rather can aid mental health. Even though she is clearly of another religious persuasion, she is respectful of the faith of those in the group, several of whom are Christians.

This is part of the reason I am not absolutely convinced that Christians must see Christian therapists. What is, after all, a Christian therapist? A Christian who happens to be a therapist? A therapist who happens to be a Christian? A therapist who uses Christian concepts, practices, and scriptures in the context of therapy? As in the case of S., a therapist of another religion can be just as supportive and understanding of religious life and experience. As in the case of C., a therapist may be religiously neutral and still able to help practicing Christians in profound ways.

Having said that, I do think that if you can find a practicing Christian therapist or therapist Christian, or at least a religious therapist with whom you feel comfortable, this would be better than engaging a secular therapist. My guess is that C. is rare in his ability and that Dr. S. is more exemplary in his incapacity to "try on" another's religious worldview. Simply, this would avoid the possible Freudian-Feuerbachian-Marxist assumptions (religion is a crutch to deal with the fact of death; religion is viewing the self writ large on the cosmic screen; religion is the opiate of the masses) of many secular therapists and psychiatrists I have known. Such a worldview may only damage the spiritual life of the Christian as well as the trust in the therapeutic relationship.

> I have set before you life and death, blessings and curses. Choose life so that you and your descendants may live, loving the Lord your God, obeying him, and holding fast to him; for that means life to you and length of days.
>
> Deuteronomy 30:19–20

If you, my reader, are feeling that you may be experiencing symptoms of mental illness (see appendix II for a quick checklist), do not wait to get help. The whole syndrome or set of symptoms may only get worse if left unaddressed. As a friend once encouraged me, don't wait until you see the whites of their eyes to shoot; you must shoot as soon as you see the red of their coats. If you or anyone you know are experiencing some of the symptoms of mental illness, seek help right away. There is so much help out there, and as the psalmist knows, praising God is our purpose in life, and "who will give you thanks in the grave?" Anything we can use to get out of the grave is a good thing.

In the end, one can view secular therapy not as a threat from the "outside" but as spoiling the gold of the Egyptians. Just as Moses and his crew were told to take from the riches of the Egyptians, so the Christian should feel unconstrained to borrow from secular wisdom in the healing of mental illnesses. The Christian should bear in mind that this spoiling of the Egyptians can be good and proper, as long as the "Egyptian" doesn't try to tear at the gold, so to speak, and mistrust, or worse yet dismantle, the religious experience and spirituality of the patient.

Therefore, when you choose a therapist, do so carefully. Interview him or her, and at least one or two others. Check out their office. What does it tell you about them? Is it neat and organized, or is it a mess? Ask about their degrees and experience in therapy. How many years' experience do they have? What do they enjoy most about their job? How do they feel about religious patients? What is their understanding of Christianity? Do they answer these questions eagerly, or do they want to know why you are asking? This last strategy can be a huge cop-out on the part of a psychotherapist. Usually it is done with the proper goal of getting you to talk more, but right now you want answers to your questions. Do they have trouble answering your questions? Do they seem to like you and make you feel comfortable? Is there a good rapport? The most important part of your work together will come from the relationship itself, so you will want to choose someone with whom you have the highest possibility for a good therapeutic relationship.

Ultimately, the best therapeutic relationship will be based on trust. This is why it depends entirely on the match between therapist and patient, rather than religious issues per se. However, if what you are looking for is someone to pray with you and to pray for you, I would advise that you seek out either clergy or a spiritual director to be another party in your therapeutic "package."

I should add a word about therapy itself. It is not an easy road. You will come to face events and facts about your life, your family, your personality, your choices, that you might rather not have to face. Rather than "feeling therapeutic," it may, especially at first, make you feel torn up inside. For example, being reminded of the anniversary of any death can be literally sickening, and this can come up in therapy: the sane mind can become clouded at the remembrance of such pain. Anniversaries of tragedies are all the more painful. The sufferer may have to take days off work and the world of busyness to recuperate. Anniversaries of suicides may be that much harder still. The remembrance of the pain of the mind and soul who took its own life never leaves you. And therapy leads you to remember and face such things.

You may have to go through a few therapists until you find one whom you can trust, with whom you feel comfortable. And if your insurance won't cover it, it can be quite expensive. Choosing against therapy for mental illness because of the expense is usually, however, more painful, more difficult, and more expensive than engaging in the therapy would have been.

As you look for a mental health professional, you may need a psychiatrist, for he or she can prescribe medicine. This professional has a medical degree, an M.D., and sometimes a Ph.D. in a medical field. You may prefer either a social worker for therapy, an LCSW (licensed clinical social worker), or a psychologist, some of whom may have more years of education than a psychiatrist, if this matters to you. These do not prescribe medicine, so if you need medicine you will also need a psychiatrist for your medical requirements. A social worker can often be less expensive and better skilled in therapy than an M.D., although this entirely depends upon the person. There are also various kinds of "counselors," some of whom may advertise themselves as Christians. They may not necessarily have a degree in therapeutic counseling, so ask. In some states, just about anybody can hang out their shingle as a "therapist."

Personally, I would not necessarily want to be seen by a Christian counselor per se; I would wonder if their version of

Christianity were really that close to mine anyhow. Sometimes the "liberal" Christian can have a worldview so different from that of the orthodox Christian that the two would make a potentially dubious match for successful therapy. Freud, Marx, and Feuerbach do not square with an orthodox understanding of Christianity. For a therapist to have a view of God so radically different from the patient's might not make for the best therapeutic relationship.

But, all things being equal, if one can find a Christian therapist who is trustworthy and has the proper training, it may be advantageous to the Christian patient to seek this out. At least you would avoid some of the difficulties I had with some of my secular psychiatrists. And being able to pray as part of a therapy session, and knowing that your therapist is praying for you, could be an outstanding feature of your therapy.

Conclusion

This is my comfort in my trouble,
that your promise gives me life. . . .
It is good for me that I have been afflicted,
that I might learn your statutes.

Psalm 119:50, 71

It is *good* for me that I have been afflicted? Isn't there an easier way to learn God's statutes? How can I agree with the psalmist here? In the midst of all my ills, there have been indeed several concrete things that I can say that I learned, that God has taught me in his mercy and despite my misery.

One of the things that God in his mercy has taught me from my illness has been about the nature of Christian marriage. Illnesses, especially mental illnessses, can either destroy a marriage or cement it. In my case my marriage was strengthened.

I remember when I married at age twenty-two that the traditional vows meant much to me. But when it came to "in sickness and in health," I always thought I was promising to take care of Matthew. It did not occur to me that I would need to be taken care of. It did not enter my mind that I might be weak someday and need to accept his love in a new way. I had never thought that life's circumstances might render us no longer equals in the give and take of unconditional love.

Of course, when we marry we cannot foresee the blessings and curses we will encounter in life. Hence the vows. Otherwise

155

it would be easy to say to ourselves that our spouse "just isn't the person I married." And of course, Matthew could have easily and with justification said that of me.

> Love's not love that alters when it alteration finds . . .
>
> Shakespeare (1564–1606)

But Matthew taught me how to accept love when I could not give it. This was a hard lesson indeed for me. He taught me of the wonders of grace, of the unconditional love of the marriage covenant. Because he hung on and was a rock-solid helpmeet to me, because he looked on tempest and was not shaken, I learned after my recovery the power of Christian marriage to bear it out to the edge of doom.

I thought, of course, when I made those vows as a relative youngster, that I knew what Shakespeare's sonnet meant about bearing it out to the edge of doom. "Are you ready, said the Master, to be crucified with me?" is an old hymn belted out lustily, with the reply that yes, Lord, we are ready. How dare we sing this, how dare we take these vows? Christian marriage is a crucible for the formation of Christ in us, with its daily crucifixions to self and its daily resurrections of love in the bonds of affection. Certainly I knew that as I earnestly made the vows that I did not fully understand the implications of what I was saying. But I am so grateful for those vows, and for the husband God gave me. We are best friends. We know now what is worth fighting over, and that is precious little. And if, God forbid, Matthew should become ill, I pray that I can be such a bulwark to him as he was to me.

Another thing I learned was a deep compassion for the sick, bedridden, and homeless that I did not have before. I always thought I was a person of deep compassion, but I see now that this was not true. Sometimes suffering is the only way to learn true compassion, true "feeling with." How, after all, can one put oneself into the shoes of another who is suffering without having suffered personally? I don't think that I would have agreed with this before. I simply thought that one could just imagine the other's hell. I no longer think this.

I realize that I could easily have been homeless, if I had not had the support of my husband. I was incapable of earning a living, incapable of the business of life, paying bills, putting together a meal. Now I look at the homeless with a new compassion and even respect. I now understand why some talk to themselves and are irritable and manic, or semi-comatose and unattractive. So many homeless are in that situation because they are addicts or mentally ill or both. How easy it would be to be mentally ill if one had the constant stress of being homeless. Though I have never been an addict or homeless, I see myself in them.

When I visit the sick, I see our mortality in illness, a mortality that we must not forget before God. One of the elderly whom I visit, a stroke patient, sometimes tries to talk, but he falls asleep readily amid the effort. His brain is sick. His mind must also be compromised. But his soul? Certainly not. That is why his son has a hard time knowing when to let go. "Is it hard to keep your eyes open, Victor?" I ask. He sleeps. How agonizingly difficult it is to be sick. He reminds me that I too will someday sleep in death, an easy memory from my own illness. I anoint him with holy oil, beseeching God the Father, God the Son, and God the Holy Spirit to grant him peace. "The grass withers, the flower fades; but the word of our God will stand forever" (Isaiah 40:8).

To mark your own mortality before the Almighty is to acknowledge his sovereignty, his abiding mercy and grace. The sovereignty of God is easy to forget when one is healthy and assumes that one has all the time in the world. "So teach us to number our days that we may apply our hearts to wisdom" (Psalm 90:12). In a sense this is what we do in our Lenten disciplines: number our days. My life these past years has been one long Lent, out of which has come a resurrection of compassion.

I also learned that sick people are not necessarily weak. Sick people are just afflicted. And they need the help of the Christian community. The mentally ill can shock people, and the stigma of mental illness can mean that people are often turned off to the sufferer. But it should be the Christian community of all places where such sufferers are welcomed and supported, prayed for and comforted.

I learned what faith means even in abandonment, especially in abandonment. Even in my very great suffering, when prayer was shouting blasphemies at God and I felt completely abandoned, somehow deep down I knew that Jesus was with me, even if in an absent way. I saw the backside of God, as Moses did hiding in the cleft of the rock. And maybe this is all I could take. After all, no one sees the face of God and lives (Ex. 33:17–23). Seeing the backside of God is incredibly painful, but at least I saw God in absence in the midst of my illness.

And even in my abandonment, I remembered even if only foggily that God had good plans for me (Jeremiah 29:11), plans for welfare and not for evil, *to give me a future and a hope.* It was painful to remember this, and I had to keep reminding myself over and over. At that time, I really did imagine God as a huge cat and I as a helpless mouse being batted back and forth by God's paws. When will God stop playing with me like this? *God has plans for your welfare and not for evil, to give you a future and a hope.* Please give me that future now, I prayed. I had to have patience when every ounce of my flesh fought for immediate health, which was denied me. Faith can be this sort of patience, a hanging on when nothing worthy of God's glory is felt or sensed. Faithfulness in this context truly makes God's face beam.

To a certain extent, therefore, I will miss my tribulations. I have not known the severe pain of my brain disorder now for over two years. However, it remains a part of my life. The analogy the doctor has given me is that my disease is like diabetes: there is no cure, but with care there is a way to treat it so that it is not fatal, terminal. I still must take my medication faithfully, avoiding the foods that interact with it. I must make sure to exercise every day, to see my therapists and doctors, to allow for this invasion into my life. Yet without the pain, I do learn less about faith, about the nature of faithfulness, about my own weaknesses and God's strength. I am so relieved, however, to have returned from among the tombs. I have my memories, which will continue to teach me.

> Why are you cast down, O my soul?
> And why are you disquieted within me?
> Hope in God; for I shall again praise him, my help and my God.
>
> Psalms 42 and 43 (RSV)

I learned during these years to pray. It was not as if I had never prayed before. As with learning compassion, which I thought I already knew, I relearned how to pray. The Daily Office helped with this, in its forms for prayer and its place for intercessory prayer. However, it was more than just this. Prayer from a mentally ill mind is exceedingly difficult. Not only is it hard to concentrate, which is necessary for prayer, it is also painful to give thanks. Which means one has to try all the harder, or maybe not at all: to let the Holy Spirit pray through you is a form of prayerful surrender.

I knew from scripture that to be faithful one had to hope in God and praise God, but how could I do that now? Not, certainly, on my own. I strapped myself to the prayers and praises of Israel, the scripture, and relied on other's prayers from ancient Israel to my present-day parish and family. We sometimes forget the importance of intercessory prayer, but we must remember that sometimes we may be praying for someone who simply cannot pray for themselves. I learned that prayer might not always feel good, that it may be more like scaling a sharp cliff than walking on smooth, level paths. But I learned that we must always pray, even and especially when we don't feel it or it feels compulsory and rote and dry.

When an acquaintance had bone cancer, his friends stood around him and exclaimed at his courage and faith. He would look shocked and say that he had no faith, no courage, that being ill did not necessarily make one virtuous. I know now how he felt. Friends would tell me what a witness I was to the grace of God. Of course I did not feel myself to be any such witness; I just knew that I had to make it through my own trials. "My brothers and sisters, whenever you face trials of any kind, consider it nothing but joy" (James 1:2).

A dear friend made me a prie-dieu for my ordination. It stands in my office, holding a prayer book and a Bible. Whenever I say prayers while kneeling at that beautiful handmade piece of art, my soul is humbled and lifted at the same time. How could anyone make such an object for me? Partly out of friendship, and partly because he knows that as a priest I have a responsibility to pray on behalf of the community of faith. Thanks be to God that through the mire and clay, now I truly can pray, and more deeply than ever before.

I also learned something very deep about the Christian life: even for all that pain, I would not give it up for what I learned through it. I had known intellectually before that joy is different from happiness, but here it was engraved on my heart. Sometimes we will be simply unhappy, and sometimes very unhappy indeed, but the joy of the LORD is our strength (Nehemiah 8:10). Joy comes not from the vicissitudes of daily circumstance as does happiness, but from the deep calling to deep, God's voice to us as we hear it in scripture and sacrament. God in his providence weaves joy into our lives despite the suffering.

> O LORD, my heart is not lifted up,
> my eyes are not raised too high.
> I do not occupy myself with things
> too great and too marvelous for me.
> But I have calmed and quieted my soul,
> like a child quieted at her mother's breast,
> like a child that is quieted is my soul.
> O Israel, hope in the LORD from this time forth and forever more.
>
> Psalm 131 (RSV)

This psalm goes from individual lament to corporate hope and praise. And this is the journey of our lives before God, proceeding from our laments to the praise and hope offered by the God of Israel, and the Israel of God. This is not sticky-sweet pabulum to compensate for the pain; it is the very life of Jesus poured out for us. Joy comes from the crucified and risen Jesus, not from our inner psyche.

This is why, as I have said, the personality matters little to our life before God. Especially when a person is mentally ill, the personality, the outward affect, changes or even dissolves. Affect and desire may change, but no matter how fickle our heart and mind are, God is constant. God is faithful even though we are changing or changed. And this is a source of joy.

I also learned that despair is not the chief sin for the mentally ill. Despair is a reaction to evil, evil as the forces that work against God's good creation and providence. Despair may even be involuntary, caused by a brain disorder; it may be voluntary, caused by giving up. But it is always a reaction to some form of evil, some deprivation of the good, and therefore understandable as such. This is an exceedingly important lesson: *despair can live with Christian faith.* Indeed, having despair while knowing in your heart that God has conquered even that is a great form of faith, for it is tried by fire.

And the counterpart to despair is hope. This kind of hope is not merely optimism, which looks to the present with a cheery face. Christian hope looks to the future, to God's promise of the resurrection, which is God's act alone, the turning around of all things to God. "If for this life only we have hoped in Christ, we are of all people most to be pitied" (1 Corinthians 15:19). It is this future that redeems our present and allows us to have hope beyond mere optimism. Hope is not a subjective feeling but an objective knowledge of God's being, act, and identity. Therefore even those with mental illnesses who cannot "feel" hope must be reassured of its objectivity—an important role for the Christian friend. "Hope that is seen is not hope" (Romans 8:24). In God's good time, in the heavenly Jerusalem there will be no more tears, for God himself will wipe them away. "Weeping may spend the night, but joy comes in the morning" (Psalm 30:6).

With the apostle Paul, who certainly had his own difficulties in his ministry, I have learned to say:

> In all these things we are more than conquerors through him who loved us. For I am convinced that neither death, nor life, nor angels, nor rulers, nor things present, nor things to come, nor powers, nor height, nor depth, nor anything else in all creation, will be able to separate us from the love of God in Christ Jesus our Lord.
>
> Romans 8:37–39

Nothing in all of creation will be able to separate us from the love of God, not death nor dwelling on death, not illness that even makes us turn away at times from God and from life. This is because we are conquerors through him who loved us, Jesus Christ. Even in the midst of mental illness, to know we are conquerors leads to health. Who says, after all, that Christian faith is a misstep toward psychological healing?

Thirteen years now after my diagnosis of major depression and seven years after my diagnosis with bipolar disorder, after good and bad times, I have now had two good years. Two years of solid improvement, working again at full steam, able to talk to people without being in pain, smiling without feeling that my face will crack. I do not anticipate the coming day with dread, nor do I fear manic episodes. I suppose all of this could recur, but I have a new confidence that if it does, it will not crush me as it did. For now it seems more like Jesus has chased it away, with the help of medicine and therapy, a loving family and supportive friends.

"See, the home of God is among mortals.
He will dwell with them as their God;
they will be his peoples
and God himself will be with them;
he will wipe away every tear from their eyes.
Death will be no more,
mourning and crying and pain will be no more,
for the first things have passed away."

And the one who was seated on the throne said, "See, I am making all things new."

Revelation 21:3–5

See, I am making all things new. This is the message of the redemption we have in Christ Jesus. There will be no more crying or pain anymore. These things have passed away, because the One who rules, who sits on the throne, has conquered it all. Of course, this happens at the end time, when Jesus comes back to reign definitively over all powers. Until then, we do have tears, we do suffer, we do confront our own death. But the promise given those in Christ is that God will make all things new beyond death, tears, and illness.

Transfiguration 2005

Appendix I

Why and How I Use Scripture

Teach me, O Lord, the way of your statutes,
and I shall keep it to the end.

Psalm 119:33

Scripture can be vitally important to the mentally ill Christian. It bears to her not only the voice and will of the triune God but also the community of faith which she cannot often see or feel immediately. Reading scripture is a discipline that at times in mental illness is almost impossible and yet remains necessary for spiritual health. Why is this so? Because scripture bears the saving grace of God. It witnesses to the God who loves and elects the unsuspecting Israel, who brings in God's victory over the powers of evil and death in the life, death, and resurrection of Jesus Christ. This back-handed working through history continues throughout scripture, which is part of the reason that we must read it again and again.

Lord, you have given us your word for a light to shine on our path.
Inspire us to meditate on that word, and follow its teaching, that

we may find in it the light which shines more and more until it is perfect day, through Jesus Christ our Lord. Amen.

Jerome (340–420)

Scripture does not tell a story we naturally know. It tells an odd story, not one that we would always and everywhere be comfortable with. It tells a story that breaks fresh from the page to witness again and again to the love of God in Jesus Christ. It surprises us again and again. This surprise of God is healing to body, mind, and spirit. And this is why we must read it again and again, every day, because each time we approach scripture it will tell us something new.

I read scripture because in it I find the Lord of life, the crucified and risen King who claims victory over all deathly powers. This is true whether I am mentally healthy or ill. But for someone who is mentally ill, encountering the Lord of life when all one can think about is death and despair is not only surprising, indeed shocking, but also healing. I found this true especially when reading the areas of the canon that I don't often read in devotions and the Daily Office, especially the corners and back passageways of the Old Testament. The psalms were also very important to me, because we read them regularly in the Daily Office. They speak very meaningfully to the one who suffers.

It is a wondrous and beneficial thing that the Holy Spirit organized the Holy Scripture so as to satisfy hunger by means of its plainer passages and remove boredom by means of its obscurer ones.

Augustine (354–430)

But how does one read scripture? Theologians such as I are trained to read scripture as historical critics, if we are trained to read scripture at all. But reading the Noah cycle and pulling apart the sources is not very edifying to the soul.[1] Questioning whether Jesus really said such and such or whether his statement is from Q or special Matthew is not very nourishing.[2] As we read

1. The Noah cycle in Genesis 6–9 is apparently composed by two authors, with their material woven together.
2. Q stands for the German *Quelle*, meaning "source." It refers to a hypothetical source of Jesus's sayings that appear in Matthew and Luke but not in Mark.

scripture, it is as though these theologically puny questions and their punier answers from much of the so-called higher biblical criticism wring out of us any interest in questions of existence and faithfulness to the God of Jesus Christ.

I follow the standard traditional practice of reading scripture against itself (*scriptura sui interpres*: scripture is its own interpreter). This was an important practice in the Reformation but can also be seen throughout the history of biblical reading. To claim that scripture is its own interpreter is not to imply that scripture needs no human interpreter. Of course, the human subject always confronts the Word with her own questions and interests. And different interpreters come up with different interpretations. I do not deny that.

But reading scripture against itself means to acknowledge the unity of the canon. I read Matthew, and then turn to Isaiah and its voice quoted in Matthew. I read Galatians, then turn to James, without throwing up my hands in despair at the seeming contradictions. The point is not to claim that Matthew misquotes Isaiah or that Galatians cancels out James or vice versa, but that by reading one text against another we learn more. We can dig out the marrow of scripture by reading it according to itself.

> Blessed Lord, who caused all holy Scriptures to be written for our learning: Grant us so to hear them, read, mark, learn and inwardly digest them, that we may embrace and ever hold fast the blessed hope of everlasting life, which you have given us in our Savior Jesus Christ; who lives and reigns with you and the Holy Spirit, one God, for ever and ever. Amen.
>
> BCP, 236

I read scripture with the traditional claim that it is inspired of God. When I find a particular "error" or "inconsistency," I question why that may appear as such, what it might tell me about the Divine Voice. I do not take such "errors" to be indicative of a lack of meaning or of scripture's having been "falsified." To say that scripture is inspired is to say that it has a purpose, it has a direction. It is not necessarily to make an argument for scripture's accuracy or textual perfection, but rather and quite simply to say that scripture is for us, *pro nobis*. In this it is not like any other text, nor is it read like any other text, although it certainly can be. But when one is at the brink of death, one reads scripture with a thirst that it will say something hopeful, promising.

I read scripture according to the Rule of Faith. In the first through third centuries, both in the Bible and among those who commented on it, there were Rules of Faith. These were somewhat like precreedal creeds, based on a trinitarian pattern, and they told the story of scripture. They were a take on scripture's whole, the understanding of those who came before orthodoxy but foreshadowed and contributed to it. These Rules were not codified by any churchly council (that came later), and they varied slightly from geographical area to area. Based on scripture's story, they were reapplied to scripture in interpretation. They yielded a set or circle of interpretations, within which interpretations were deemed to be faithful and outside of which they were not. Irenaeus (125–202) uses the analogy of a mosaic: just as there is a pattern that governs the way the tiles of a mosaic are put together, so there is a pattern to scripture's interpretation. Irenaeus then uses another illustration: one can use the same tiles to put together a mosaic of the king or, using another pattern, a mosaic of a dog. The rule of faith, or rule of truth, is the church's "pattern" to render the portrait of the King. Augustine (354–430) later came up with a guide to interpretation which I also follow: the Rule of Love. Using both the Rule of Faith and Rule of Love, one may come up with any interpretation that does not contradict the faith of scripture or the love of God and neighbor.

I read the Old and New Testaments as one canon. That is, I do not say to myself, *That Old Testament is just so barbaric and adolescent, I will just not pay attention to what it says.* The Old Testament bears the hope of Israel just as the New Testament bears the hope of the church. It bears the Word just as much (if not arguably more) than the New Testament. When I come across a difficult passage in the Old Testament, or in the New for that matter, I struggle with it until I can gain some meaning out of it. If I still can't, I am willing to leave it alone until I am wiser, should such a day ever come, rather than jettisoning it in my mind as though it were less profound than I. I understand those who came before me to have been the giants on whose shoulders we now sit, as we hope for even better vision than they had, but not apart from them.

If you cannot yet understand, you should leave the matter for
the consideration of those who can; and since Scripture does not
abandon you in your infirmity, but with a mother's love accom-
panies your slower steps, you will make progress. Holy Scripture,
indeed, speaks in such a way as to mock the proud readers with
its heights, terrify the attentive with its depths, feed great souls
with its truth and nourish little ones with sweetness.

Augustine (354–430)

I read scripture as though it speaks afresh to today as well as
it spoke to yesterday. It is directed not only to those of Israel and
the Jesus communities but also to our contemporary context. This
is another way in which scripture is unlike many other historical texts. When I read the psalms, for example, I read them as
speaking to my own situation. They comfort me: "LORD, you have
searched me out and known me; you know my sitting down and
my rising up. . . . Where can I go then from your Spirit? where
can I flee from your presence?" (Psalm 139). They humble me:
"Against you and you alone have I sinned" (Psalm 51). They
make me sing with joy: "Bless the LORD, O my soul, and all that
is within me, bless his holy Name" (Psalm 103).

To allow scripture to speak afresh today, I have learned from
early and medieval biblical interpretation not to be limited to one
"sense," one meaning, in the scriptures. In early and medieval
biblical interpretation, interpreters often read first the literal
sense of the passage, then the spiritual senses. This included the
tropological or moral sense; then the allegorical sense or what
you should believe; and the anagogical sense, or the eschatologi-
cal or future sense. The classic illustration here is as follows:
Jerusalem is according to the literal sense a city in the Near
East; while according to the tropological sense it is the human
heart; according to the allegorical sense it is the church; and
according to the anagogical sense it is the Heavenly City. This
is never a rigid plan for early and medieval exegesis, nor am I
suggesting that it should be for us now. This too is a departure
from the "program" of higher criticism, which should be obvious.
But I find it quite fruitful, especially when reading the psalms
or any other text of scripture devotionally. After all, the psalms
can seem bloodthirsty and violent at times (e.g., Psalm 137).
How can one read that psalm or similar psalms devotionally

unless by transmuting the Babylonian babies, or the enemies, into something else? So when I read the psalms, my enemies according to the tropological sense were my mood swings, my brain chemistry, thoughts and feelings that were beyond my control and were truly my enemies. Many people feel turned off by the warlike imagery of the Old Testament, but how many of us have figurative yet very real enemies that we need to fight and bring to peace under the authority of God!

In addition, acknowledging that scripture speaks on different levels allows us to read Christ as the speaker of the psalms. It is he who says, "Pray for the peace of Jerusalem" (Psalm 122), and it is he who says, "My God, my God, why have you forsaken me?" (Psalm 22; Mark 15:34; Matthew 27:46). Throughout its history the church has understood Christ to be the speaker of the psalms. Reading scripture on different levels of meaning breaks open the historical-critical stranglehold and allows for creative and faithfully meaningful readings.

I also read scripture as a daughter of the church. This brings us back to the Rule of Faith in one sense: I would never knowingly offer an interpretation that could damage the church or the faith of any of its "little ones." On the other hand this brings us into the community of the present, my parish, my diocese, my communion. Past and present, and not only this but future. And this brings us back to the notion of the different senses of scripture, in its anagogical sense referring to the Heavenly City and its banquet. To read scripture as a daughter of the church is never to offer an interpretation that contradicts the life of faith. Of course this is tricky, as different people have differing opinions as to what harms or contradicts the life of faith in the body of Christ.

And this is where community comes in. At different points along the way, I have been part of prayer and Bible study groups, intimate groups in which we studied scripture together. Ultimately scripture is not to be read alone but in the context of the church, either the body gathered on Sundays where it is proclaimed, "This is the Word of the Lord," or midweek in small groups. In small groups members can offer various potential readings of scripture. The community offers of its own, just as during the Sunday sermon the preacher offers her own.

This is why in this book, in addition to scripture, I have included prayers and sayings from other Christians throughout the history of the church. Even when I felt that darkness was my only companion, I could gain nourishment and holy friendship from those who came before me. Knowing that they experienced their own sufferings and yet were able to praise God was a great source of strength to me. The community throughout the ages was a source of courage. "Therefore, since we are surrounded by so great a cloud of witnesses, let us also lay aside every weight and the sin which clings so closely, and let us run with perseverance the race that is set before us, looking to Jesus the pioneer and perfecter of our faith" (Hebrews 12:1).

Appendix II

A Brief Checklist of Symptoms and Resources

Symptoms of Depression

A person has five or more of the following symptoms over a two-week period, or the symptoms interfere with that person's life[1]:

Feeling sad, crying more than usual
Major changes in appetite or sleep patterns
Uncharacteristic irritability, anger
Worries, anxieties
Pessimism, feelings of failure
Loss of energy, libido
Unexplained physical aches and pains
Hopelessness, guilt
Inability to concentrate or make decisions
Inability to carry out personal hygiene (showering, brushing teeth, etc.)

1. The first two sets of symptoms in this checklist have been adapted from material put out by the Depression and Bipolar Support Alliance.

Lack of enjoyment in things formerly enjoyed
No desire to socialize
Recurring thoughts of death or suicide

Symptoms of Mania

Three or more of the following symptoms for two weeks or more, or which interfere with the person's life:

Increased physical and mental activity and energy
Extreme optimism and self-confidence
Exalted sense of self-importance
Irritability, aggressiveness
Decreased need for sleep
Pressured speech and thoughts
Impulsiveness and reckless behavior (spending money, driving, sex, etc.)
Delusions (thinking things that aren't real or true) and hallucinations (seeing things that aren't there)

Symptoms of Schizophrenia

Two of the five following symptoms present over the course of at least one month[2]:

Delusions
Hallucinations
Disorganized speech
Grossly disorganized behavior, or catatonia
Blunting of personality or affect and blunting of will or drive

(Some of these may be present in severe depression or mania)

2. These are taken from J. Raymond DePaulo and Leslie Alan Horvitz DePaulo, *Understanding Depression: What We Know and What You Can Do about It* (New York: John Wiley & Sons, 2002), 55.

The following organizations and websites may be of some interest and help as you go about seeking therapy:

Depression After Delivery
800-944-4773
www.infotrail.com/dad/

Post-Partum Support International
www.postpartum.net

National Alliance for the Mentally Ill
200 Glebe Road, Suite 1015
Arlington, VA 22203-3754
Phone: 703-524-7600
Fax: 703-524-9094
www.nami.org

National Mental Health Association
800-969-6642
www.nmha.org

Depression and Bipolar Support Alliance
800-826-3632
www.DBSAlliance.org

Miscellaneous websites
www.bipolar.about.com
www.psychiatry24x7.com

You can ask the brothers of Taizé, the ecumenical monastery in France, to keep you in their prayers. Their website is www.taize.fr. To request prayer, go to the website, click Prayer and Song, go to the sidebar, and click Prayer Intentions.

When you are too sick to leave the house, you can still say the Daily Office "with others" on the Web. Go to www.mission stclare.com.

Bibliography

The Autobiography of a Schizophrenic Girl: The True of Story of "Renée." New York: Penguin Group, 1968.

Bauby, Jean-Dominique. *The Diving Bell and the Butterfly: A Memoir of Life in Death.* New York: Random House, 1997.

Benner, David G., ed. *Christian Counseling and Psychotherapy.* Grand Rapids: Baker, 1987.

Brown, Warren S., Nancey Murphy and H. Newton Malony. *Whatever Happened to the Soul? : Scientific and Theological Portraits of Human Nature.* Minneapolis: Fortress, 1998.

Calvin, John. *Institutes of the Christian Religion.* Philadelphia: Westminster, 1960.

Casey, Nell, ed. *Unholy Ghost: Writers on Depression.* New York: Harper Collins, 2001.

Cronkite, Kathy. *On the Edge of Darkness: Conversations about Conquering Depression.* New York: Doubleday, 1994.

DePaulo, J. Raymond and Leslie Alan Horvitz. *Understanding Depression: What We Know and What You Can Do about It.* New York: John Wiley & Sons, 2002.

Dossey, Larry. *Healing Words: The Power of Prayer and the Practice of Medicine.* New York: HarperPaperbacks, 1993.

Fawcett, Jan, and Bernard Golden. *New Hope for People with Bipolar Disorder.* Roseville, CA: Prima Health, 2000.

Flanagan, Owen. *The Problem of the Soul: Two Visions of Mind and How to Reconcile Them*. New York: Basic Books, 2002.

Green, Joel B., and Stuart Palmer, ed. *In Search of the Soul: Four Views of the Mind-Body Problem*. Downers Grove, IL: InterVarsity Press, 2005.

Heckler, Richard A. *Waking Up, Alive: The Descent, the Suicide Attempt, and the Return to Life*. New York: Ballantine Books, 1994.

Heisler, Susan L. *Anthology of a Crazy Lady: A Creative Cure Through Writing and Art*. Newark, DE: Victoria Publishing, 2000.

Hobson, J. Allan. "Neuroscience and the Soul: The Dualism of John Carew Eccles." *Cerebrum* 6:2 (Spring 2004): 61–70.

Hunsinger, Deborah van Deusen. *Theology and Pastoral Counseling: A New Interdisciplinary Approach*. Grand Rapids: Eerdmans, 1994.

Jamison, Kay Redfield, *Touched with Fire: Manic-Depressive Illness and the Artistic Temperament*. New York: Free Press, 1993.

___. *An Unquiet Mind: A Memoir of Moods and Madness*. 1995. New York: Vintage Books, 1996.

___. *Night Falls Fast: Understanding Suicide*. New York: Alfred A. Knopf, 1999.

Jones, Stanton L., and Richard E. Butman. *Modern Psycho-Therapies: A Comprehensive Christian Appraisal*. Downers Grove, IL: InterVarsity Press, 1991.

Karp, David A., *Speaking of Sadness: Depression, Disconnection and the Meaning of Illness*. New York: Oxford University Press, 1996.

___. *The Burden of Sympathy: How Families Cope with Mental Illness*. New York: Oxford University Press, 2001.

Kaysen, Susannah, *Girl, Interrupted*. New York: Vintage Books, 1993.

Keck, David. *Forgetting Whose We Are*. Nashville: Abingdon, 1996.

Lloyd-Jones, D. Martyn. *Spiritual Depression: Its Causes and Cure*. Grand Rapids: Eerdmans, 1965.

Lowenthal, David. *The Past is a Foreign Country*. Cambridge: Cambridge University Press, 1985.

Manning, Martha. *Undercurrents: A Therapist's Reckoning with Her Own Depression*. San Francisco: HarperSanFranciso, 1994.

Marsh, Diane T., and Rex Dickens. *How to Cope with Mental Illness in Your Family: A Self-Care Guide for Siblings, Offspring, and Parents*. New York: Penguin Putnam, 1997.

Martyn, Dorothy. *The Man in the Yellow Hat*. Atlanta: Scholar's Press, 1992.

Mondimore, Francis Mark. *Bipolar Disorder: A Guide for Patients and Families*. Baltimore: Johns Hopkins, 1999.

Neugeboren, Jay. *Transforming Madness: New Lives for People Living with Mental Illness*. New York: William Morrow & Co., 1999.

Papoulos, Demitri, and Janice Papoulos. *The Bipolar Child: The Definitive and Reassuring Guide to Childhood's Most Misunderstood Disorder*. New York: Broadway Books, 1999.

Pascal, Blaise, *Pensées: The Provincial Letters*. The Modern Library. New York: Random House, 1941.

Pauley, Jane. *Skywriting: A Life Out of the Blue*. New York: Random House, 2004.

Paul, Pamela. "The Power to Uplift." *Time*, 17 January 2005, A46–A48.

Phillips, Timothy R., & Mark R. McMinn, ed. *Care for the Soul: Exploring the Intersection of Psychology and Theology*. Downers Grove, IL: InterVarsity, 2001.

Plath, Sylvia, *The Bell Jar*. 1971. New York: Harper & Collins, 1996.

Propst, R. *Psychotherapy in a Religious Framework: Spirituality in the Emotional Healing Process*. New York: Human Sciences Press, 1988.

Rittgers, Ronald K. "Martin Luther and the 'Christian Art of Suffering.'" Unpublished paper, 2004.

Sacks, Oliver, *The Man Who Mistook His Wife For a Hat and Other Clinical Tales*. 1970. New York: Touchstone, 1998.

Schneidman, Edwin S. *The Suicidal Mind*. New York: Oxford University Press, 1996.

Searle, John R. *The Rediscovery of the Mind*. Cambridge, MA: MIT Press, 1992.

Sifton, Elisabeth. *The Serenity Prayer: Faith and Politics in Times of Peace and War*. New York: W. W. Norton, 2003.

Skoglund, Elizabeth. *Coping: Insights from Amy Carmichael, C. S. Lewis, Charles Spurgeon, Hudson Taylor, How Famous Christians Lived with Depression, Imperfection, Suffering and Need*. Glendale, CA: Regal Books, 1979.

Solomon, Andrew. *The Noonday Demon: An Atlas of Depression*. New York: Scribner, 2001.

Stackhouse, John G. *Can God Be Trusted?: Faith and the Challenge of Evil*. New York: Oxford University Press, 1998.

Styron, William. *Darkness Visible: A Memoir of Madness*. New York: Vintage Books, 1990.

Swinburne, Richard. *The Evolution of the Soul*. Oxford: Oxford University Press/Clarendon, 1986.

Tileston, Mary. *Great Souls at Prayer: Fourteen Centuries of Prayer, Praise and Aspiration from St. Augustine to Christina Rosetti and Robert Louis Stevenson*. London: Allenson & Co., 1898.

Wahl, Otto F., *Telling is Risky Business: Mental Health Consumers Confront Stigma*. Piscataway, NJ: Rutgers University Press, 1999.

Warnock, Mary. *Memory*. London: Faber and Faber, 1987.

Winerip, Michael. *9 Highland Road: Sane Living for the Mentally Ill*. New York: Vintage Books, 1994.

Wolterstorff, Nicholas. *Lament for a Son*. Grand Rapids: Eerdmans, 1987.

Worthington, Everett L., ed. *Psychotherapy and Religious Values*. Grand Rapids: Baker, 1993.

Yarhouse, Mark A., Richard E. Butman and Barrett W. McCray. *Modern Psychopathologies: A Comprehensive Christian Appraisal*. Downers Grove, IL: InterVarsity Press, 2005.